Praise for

BILLIONAIRE CAB DRIVER

"*Billionaire Cab Driver* is an excellent read and makes the often confusing topic of financial investing easily understood, even to those without any previous financial investing experience. Following the steps of Mr. Langston as he interviews Akamai Kane while he explains his simple rules of happiness and financial success is both entertaining and enlightening. Finally, the author's explanation of the value of current dollars versus future dollars and actual inflation was simple, concise, and elegantly stated. I recommend that anyone with an interest in providing for their future financial security should read a copy of *Billionaire Cab Driver*."

— SANFORD E. WARREN, JR., PARTNER AT WARREN RHOADES LLP

"In this clever book, a cab driver takes the reader on a ride through the financial world, navigating the ups and downs of investing in today's complicated market. Along the journey, the cab driver reveals himself and his life lessons, sharing clear financial advice. This guy deserves a huge tip. *Billionaire Cab Driver* is a tale for investors of all ages and experience levels, ideal for those who want to protect and grow their financial assets. I'm hailing this cab driver and rereading the book."

—JEFF ABRAMS, ATTORNEY AND MEDIATOR

"When a cab driver on a small remote island turns out to be a billionaire, you can't imagine the life lessons that are conveyed to a writer sent to capture this story: amazing, informative, educational, and life lessons we should all follow. Jody Tallal's book is truly inspiring."

—TOM EIFLER, JR. PRESIDENT, EIFLER ADVISORY GROUP

"*Billionaire Cab Driver* is replete with insights into the merits of clearly defined financial goals and how executing well-defined plans can achieve them. Jody Tallal is a diamond-hard writer, creating a diamond-clear path for readers to develop plans to maximize the value of their current earnings in a fresh and reportorial manner. Strategies that compound returns by incorporating savings strategies into financial plans is absolutely brilliant and overlooked by most experts. The examples used throughout the book demonstrate the dynamic nature of planning and importance of recognizing the economic and operational environment of each investment within a portfolio."

—JAMES J. FRIDL, PRESIDENT CROSS MARKETING, INC.

"Billionaire Cab Driver is a fun unique journey of Dan, a newspaper staff writer mentored by a successful Polynesian on the keys to financial success plus what's important in life. Dan's mission was to get the interview yet what he received was beyond all expectations. Take your own journey with the cab driver and learn the steps for exceeding your financial goals and how to enjoy life. I've personally reevaluated how I look at my finances as well as at life."

—MICHAEL DAVIS, PRESIDENT CAPITAL DISTRIBUTING, INC.

"By composing an interesting story and cleverly incorporating sophisticated financial concepts in a very readable narrative, Mr. Tallal has created a delightful and very informative experience. Presenting a readily understandable tale containing the concepts of future value of debt, income, assets and the effects of inflation, the work is both very readable and thought provoking. Further, he has added some specific recommendations and sources to pursue to become your own *Billionaire Cab Driver.* I strongly recommend this book."

—PATRICK W. PEAVY, M.D., EXECUTIVE VICE PRESIDENT O'BRIEN ENERGY COMPANY

"The author came up with a clever way to tackle the topic of financial planning and wealth building. Having been forced to start over myself at thirty-eight years old and building a successful business over the last quarter century, I found *Billionaire Cab Driver* to be an insightful read and right on the money to creating and then enjoying a meaningful life. It should be required reading in colleges, business schools and by anyone of any means aspiring to break the mold of living paycheck to paycheck."

—JOEL RAY, CEO NEW BENEFITS

"After reading *Billionaire Cab Driver*, I was struck with the realization that what I have thought about investing, wealth development, and protection has been completely wrong. As a successful surgeon, I have prided myself on the knowledge of my profession but realize after the teachings of "a simple cab driver," that a different expertise is needed for investing. Many of us think—"I am smart enough to do this on my own" or "there is no way I make enough to save and invest." Learning to apply the Rule of 72 and the 80/20 Rule can help you throw conventional money management theorems into the waste bin and move forward on a journey to increased wealth and self-sufficiency. I challenge you—no I dare you—to read this short, simple book. You have nothing to lose and everything to gain."

–JEFFREY WHITMAN, M.D., PRESIDENT AND CHIEF SURGEON, KEY-WHITMAN EYE CENTER

"A creative approach for investment planning and strategies. "The golden rule of investing reminds readers that careful research should be the highest priority for both novice and seasoned investors. An impressive educational storyline that is entertaining, informative, and motivational."

–MILES WOODALL, III, CEO VENT-A-HOOD, LTD

"It was with pleasure that I read *Billionaire Cab Driver* by Jody Tallal. This is a book that explains the core principals of how to accumulate wealth. However, unlike most books that seek to impart this data, Mr. Tallal's book does it in very logical and easy to understand steps. When you finish the book, you will see that you can implement the data and improve your financial future."

–STEVE HAYES, CHAIRMAN AMERICANS FOR FAIR TAXATION

"With 95 percent of Americans failing to provide adequately for their retirement, we all need this book. Through the interesting story of cab driver, a blueprint for financial success is laid out for the reader. I highly recommend this book to anyone who wants to jumpstart their financial planning program."

–LISA ROBERTS, PRESIDENT MILLENNIUM MANAGEMENT GROUP, LLC

"The *Billionaire Cab Driver* is an entertaining and quick read exposing the myth that there are no secretes to wealth accumulation. Rather it chronicles a series of tales around a series of disciplined strategies that anyone can embrace in their quest of financial success."

–BILL HIDELL, PRINCIPAL, HIDELL AND ASSOCIATES ARCHITECT

Billionaire

CAB DRIVER

TIMELESS LESSONS FOR FINANCIAL SUCCESS

* * * * * * * * * * *

JODY TALLAL

 WND Books

Billionaire Cab Driver

Published by WND Books, Washington, D.C. WND Books is a registered trademark of WorldNetDaily.com, Inc. ("WND")

Book designed by Mark Karis

WND Books are available at special discounts for bulk purchases. WND Books also publishes books in electronic formats. For more information call (541) 474-1776, e-mail orders@wndbooks.com, or visit www.wndbooks.com.

Paperback ISBN: 978-1-944229-68-9
eBook ISBN: 978-1-944229-69-6

Library of Congress Cataloging-in-Publication Data
Names: Tallal, Joseph J., 1951- author.
Title: Memoirs of a billionaire cab driver : lessons for a wise and secure
life / Jody Tallal.
Description: Washington, D.C. : WND Books, [2017] | Includes bibliographical
references and index.
Identifiers: LCCN 2016043642 (print) | LCCN 2016053041 (ebook) | ISBN
9781944229689 (pbk.) | ISBN 9781944229696 (ebook) | ISBN 9781944229696
(e-book)
Subjects: LCSH: Finance, Personal.
Classification: LCC HG179 .T345 2017 (print) | LCC HG179 (ebook) | DDC
332.024--dc23
LC record available at https://lccn.loc.gov/2016043642

Printed in the United States of America
17 18 19 20 21 LBM 9 8 7 6 5 4 3 2 1

To my wife Peggy, the children of our combined families, and our twelve grandchildren, who make life such a rich experience

Contents

The
Dallas Times Tribune

CABBY TURNS OUT TO BE BILLIONAIRE!!

KIKI LOA—Today, on the tiny island of Kiki Loa, a local cab driver named Akamai Kane, wrote a personal check for $15,000,000 to build a water plant for his fellow islanders. Further investigation reveals that Mr. Kane is currently worth over $20 billion, making him one of the wealthiest men in the world. The question on everybody's mind is how did a cab driver on this poor little Pacific island become one of the richest men in the world?

It appears that a major hotel corporation was considering the island for a new resort, but would not commit to it unless the island built a $15 million desalinization plant . . .

Preface

It is interesting to note that we do not receive any form of financial education in school: nothing about money, how it works, or how to become successful financially. We do learn about a great many other things in school, but without this important foundational knowledge about personal finance, the chances of having a bright financial future are significantly diminished.

I started working in the field of personal financial in 1971, before the personal financial planning industry got started. I was hired and trained by a gentleman who was working with physicians and attorneys, helping them benefit from recent tax law changes in 1969, which coincided with a recent shift by the IRS in its stance against the right of professionals to incorporate and enjoy the tax-reacted benefits an incorporated business enjoys. We called ourselves *personal financial managers.*

One of the greatest benefits I received in the process of working with my clients was being able to learn from their previous experiences. As my clients shared their past financial successes and failures with me (the vast majority of which were failures), they could always show me why things turned out the way they did based on their later evaluation of them. This after-the-fact scrutiny enabled them to see things not visible to them at the time they made their original decisions. They say hindsight is 20/20, but this is particularly true when it comes to personal finance.

The value of witnessing my clients' cumulative experiences gave me a unique perspective from which to see things and further develop my philosophies about proper personal financial management. This ultimately revealed what I call the *science of personal financial management.*

One thing that became readily apparent during this period was that a high income did not proportionally equate to financial success. To the contrary, it almost seemed that making more money for many became a bigger shovel with which to dig a bigger hole.

Over time, I realized that professionals drastically needed to receive some form of personal financial education during their college years. Their education was training them for a profession that would make them significant incomes, yet they had no idea of what to do with that income to become financially successful.

In the mid 1970s I approached the University of Texas Southwestern Medical School in Dallas about creating a course for graduating seniors on personal financial management. This course was so successful the first year that it was extended to the interns and house staff at Parkland Hospital the following year.

Next, the A. Webb Roberts Center for Continuing Education at Baylor Medical School decided to offer a one-day workshop I developed around the SWMS course material to practicing physicians with a Category 1 continuing medical education credit. The success of that course led to similar courses I developed for Tulane Medical School and University of Tennessee Health Sciences Medical School.

During this time with the medical schools, I had two books published, titled *The Multimillion Dollar Discovery* (1978) and *Charting Your Course to Financial Independence* (Dallas Pub., 1983). One thing I learned through the process of writing those two books is that no matter what you try to do to spice it up, a book on personal financial planning is a dry subject, and not a fun read.

In 1985 I retired from my personal financial planning practice as one of the most successful financial planners in the country at that time. I had more millions in personal net worth than I was years old, so I retired to manage my investments. However, my personal financial education was far from over.

A few years after my retirement, the Texas economy went into a severe recession that ended up becoming a real depression. Every major bank in the state went bankrupt except for one, in San Antonio. The oil, cattle, and real estate industries (the three other primary legs to Texas economy) were similarly decimated. During that period, since all of my investments were in Texas-based real estate, I was wiped out as well.

By 1995 I was literally starting over again, but this time

with a completely new perspective about personal financial management and what it meant. What I learned in that process of losing everything was that there is another very important, hidden secret in the *science of personal financial management* that was not visible during the acquisition stage of achieving success. That secret was the importance of creating an *endgame* so you will know when it is time to quit playing.

All financial goals can be defined in concrete numbers (the total assets needed to be able to retire at a desired lifestyle, how much you need to give your children the type of education you desire them to receive, the size of the estate you want to leave to your future generation(s) to ensure their financial security, and so on). Therefore, you need to know how much in assets is required to achieve your endgame so that once you have achieved that number, you can throw your hands up in victory and quit playing the game. If you do not know what that endgame is, you will continue playing the game. This exposes you to the risks associated with investing, which could cost you everything.

Fortunately, I was able to retire again in 1999, and this time with a much greater degree of success. After my second retirement, I continued to think about the new lessons I had learned that were so critical to true financial security, and decided I wanted to share those in another book. However, from my past experience in writing on the subject of personal financial planning, I knew that this new book needed to be something unique and different to engage readers while teaching these important lessons.

Two authors I have always admired are Og Mandino (*The Greatest Salesman in the World*) and George S. Clason (*The Richest Man in Babylon*), because they used fun-to-read *stories* to teach important life lessons as readers followed the characters' developments. *Billionaire Cab Driver* follows this same process and hopefully will accomplish similar results for you as you learn through the imaginary life story of Akamai Kane how he went from a poor boy from a small island to a cab driver worth $20 billion. Fictitious reporter Dan Langston wins the right to right to interview this amazing cabbie and learns some invaluable financial lessens along the way.

Billionaire

CAB DRIVER

1

THE STORY

My name is Dan Langston, and I am a staff writer for a large Northeastern newspaper. I was selected to write this book from more than three thousand professional writers who competed for this privilege.

Why did we all want this job so bad? It was because one of the richest men in the world had agreed to share his secrets for building personal wealth through this book. For me the motivation was simple: I was the world's worst at handling money. I felt that maybe if I got the job, some of his knowledge might rub off during the interviews. I mean, maybe he could actually teach me how to do more than just spend every dime I earn as soon as I earned it. In my wildest dreams I could never have imagined what an understatement that would turn out to be.

Before I go much further, let me back up and tell you how all this came about. It all started a little over a year ago on a tiny island in the North Pacific, called Kiki Loa. This island paradise is located approximately seventeen hundred miles due west from the Hawaiian island of Maui.

Kiki Loa is one of the most beautiful islands in the world. It is six miles wide at its widest point and a little over twelve miles long. The beaches are some of the most spectacular I have ever seen. The whole southern side of the island is a mountain that comes jutting straight up out of the ocean. It looks just like the volcano drawings from my daughter's second grade science book.

But the sunsets are what really make Kiki Loa one of the world's true vacation treasure spots. Six out of every seven days a year, you can stand anywhere along the island's west beach and see the most phenomenal sunsets you have ever seen in your life, with splashes of red, magenta, orange, pink, gold, and purple on the backdrop of a darkening sky. And if you are really lucky, you might see what the islanders call *Okue milahi aloahia*, which means the "giant green flash," a phenomenon that occurs when the sky is crystal clear at the exact moment of the sunset. To see the okue milahi aloahia, you have to stare at the point where the sun meets the ocean as the sun sets. If you don't blink, at the precise second the top of the sun disappears below the water, you will see the most brilliant flash of green light you can imagine. It is truly exhilarating.

Unfortunately, the island of Kiki Loa is very poor. Its few residents rely on farming as their primary source of income. Forty-nine out of fifty islanders are farmers with their principal crop being sugarcane. Working the sugarcane fields is a very difficult life for the farmers, and things have been getting progressively worse because the price for sugarcane has been falling since US farmers began using more productive farming techniques to grow sugar beets.

The remaining one out of fifty islanders work in the island's tourism trade, which is extremely meager, to put it politely. Tourism should have been big business for Kiki Loa, but unfortunately there are no large hotels to attract the volume of tourists needed to support the island. Up until six months ago, all Kiki Loa had was a few small bed-and-breakfasts that attracted a handful of adventurous tourists who were willing to come to a small remote island not really knowing what they would find once they got there.

About a year ago, a very large hotel corporation came to Kiki Loa to investigate building a world-class resort. Obviously, the island was bubbling with excitement. This would mean the islanders could give up their torturous lifestyle of working the sugarcane fields and have a chance for their children to have a brighter future. Everyone dreamed of how wonderful it would be if the hotel chain decided to build on Kiki Loa.

The hotel's site evaluation team was amazed at the island's natural beauty. It seemed to have it all: lush rain forests, spectacular scenery, fantastic snorkeling or scuba diving in the aqua-colored reefs of the island's northeast corner, and of course, Kiki Loa's magnificent white sandy beaches, with their remarkable sunsets. The team found everything perfect—except one thing: the island did not have a large enough freshwater supply to support the size project the company wanted to build.

The site evaluation team returned to their corporate offices to try to make the project work. However, no matter how hard they tried, they could not justify the extra $15 million it would take to build the freshwater desalinization plant required to support the hotel project.

After several months of eager anticipation, the residents of Kiki Loa were informed that unless they could commit to building their own desalinization plant within sixty days, the hotel would choose another island for the project. The entire island was devastated. This was their one ticket to a better, more prosperous life for their families.

Everyone was talking about the problem and trying to come up with a solution. Day after day the talks continued. As the sixty-day deadline neared, a great weight seemed to settle over the entire island as its people finally accepted the reality that their dream was about to vanish.

Then, two days before the deadline, the most amazing thing happened. Akamai Kane, the island's only taxi driver, came forth and wrote a personal check for $15 million to pay for the water plant. At first people thought he was playing a joke, trying to lighten up a sad situation. After all, he was such a good-natured old gentleman and always seemed to know what to do. Besides, how could a cab driver afford to write a check for $15 million? But to everyone's amazement, the check was good, and so began the most fantastic story I have ever reported.

I won't bore you with the details, but it was soon discovered that Akamai Kane was one of the richest men in the world, and no one had known it. How could *that* be? He was a native Kiki Loaean; the birth records proved that. Yet, nobody on Kiki Loa had ever earned any real money, so the questioned was, how did *he* do it? Everybody wanted an answer.

It didn't take long before the story hit the media. I can still remember reading the first story as it came off the wire:

CABBY TURNS OUT TO BE BILLIONAIRE!!

Kiki Loa—Today, on the tiny island of Kiki Loa, a local cab driver named Akamai Kane, wrote a personal check for $15,000,000 to build a water plant for his fellow islanders. Further investigation reveals that Mr. Kane is currently worth over $20 billion, making him one of the wealthiest men in the world. The question on everybody's mind is how did a cab driver on this poor little Pacific island become one of the richest men in the world?

It appears that a major hotel corporation was considering the island for a new resort, but would not commit to it unless the island built a $15 million desalinization plant . . .

How did a cab driver get $20 billion? I couldn't believe it! I immediately grabbed the phone and got an international operator. What I found out over the next two days was that it was impossible to reach Akamai Kane. It soon became apparent that I wasn't the only journalist who wanted to find him.

During the next week I tried everything, but without success. Mr. Kane was refusing any kind of interview. I guess I really can't blame the guy; just about every reporter in the world must have been trying to talk to him.

Then a spokesperson for Mr. Kane announced that he was flattered by all the attention and everyone's interest, but that he didn't want to spend all his time answering the same questions repeatedly. As a solution, he said that he had decided to let one journalist, whom he would select from applications submitted, write his life's story. To enter the selection process, each journalist should submit, in that writer's own opinion, his or her finest work.

I made up my mind at that very moment that I wanted to be the one who told Akamai Kane's personal story. In fact, it surprised me just how much I wanted to be selected—more than anything I have ever wanted in my life.

I instantly knew which piece I was going to submit. It wasn't either of the two war stories for which I have received my highest recognition. It was a story I wrote very early in my career, when I was still reporting for the *Boise Tribune*.

The story was about a small farming community outside Boise, Idaho, that was crippled by the drought of 1982. The crops were already severely damaged when the rains finally came. However, during a rainstorm, lightning struck one of the farmers' homes, and it burned to the ground. The other farmers worked all day long trying to save what they could of their crops, and then took shifts each evening, chipping in to rebuild their neighbor's home. It was a remarkable story about the strength and security that comes from being a community. It reminded me of something straight out of the 1800s. That story didn't win me any awards, but it did get me my current job.

I carefully packaged that story along with a very personal letter to Mr. Kane in which I sincerely shared my intense desire to be selected. I had a tough time trying to decide if my cover letter should state my true feelings or contain something clever, chock-full of wit, to display my writing style. I was afraid he might think my real motives were too selfish or dumb, but in the end I decided that honesty is the best policy.

Seven weeks went by, and I had just about concluded that

someone else must have gotten the job. Then one day, while I was sitting at my desk, the phone rang and it was Mr. Kane himself. He said he had just one question for me to answer: was I serious when I said in my letter to him that I wanted to be selected more than anything else I had ever wanted in my life? I assured him I was.

"Mr. Langston," he said, "you have the job. Will you please come to Kiki Loa at your earliest convenience?"

Shocked, I answered, "Sure, I'll be there tomorrow, and—"

"Thank you, Mr. Langston," he cut in politely. "I look forward to meeting with you in person. Good-bye." Then he hung up.

I was dumbfounded. I had just been selected from more than three thousand of the top writers in the world, all who had competed hard for this story. I realized then that I was no longer sitting; I must have instinctively stood up when I realized who was on the phone. I shook my head to make sure I wasn't dreaming and then grabbed my chair and yanked it under me just as my legs gave way. I collapsed in the chair, out of breath and experiencing the most incredible adrenaline rush of my life. I didn't move again for what seemed like an hour.

The next morning, I left at 5:45 on the first flight out for San Francisco, which connected with another flight to Hawaii. Because Kiki Loa is such a small island, no commercial airlines served it. Therefore, I had to charter a plane in Honolulu to get from there to Kiki Loa.

I got there around 9:00 p.m. and called for a taxi from the small airport to take me to the Malihini Hale, a small inn on the island. To my surprise, my taxi driver was none other than Akamai Kane himself. During the ride to the hotel, I learned that he had the only taxicab on the island, and the Malihini Hale was the only inn.

Akamai Kane was in his sixties and of Polynesian decent. He had bronze skin and large, dark eyes with a head of jet-black hair beginning to lightly streak with gray. He was a robust but gentle man who seemed to possess the secrets of youth. Being with him seemed more like being with a thirty-year-old than with someone in his sixties. He possessed a quiet sort of energy and seemed to radiate a real enthusiasm about life.

Mr. Kane informed me on my ride to the Malihini Hale that he would spend only one day with me and that he preferred doing the interview as he drove around the island in his cab. I was flabbergasted! How could I write this incredible story with only a one-day interview? When I started to protest, Mr. Kane slowed the car to a stop. He turned to me, and with a gentle smile said, "I will tell you all you need to know tomorrow. I will pick you up at 4:30 a.m. Please get out now; this is where you are staying."

I opened the car door, still spinning with confusion and anxiety, and got out of the cab. Then Mr. Kane got out of the cab and came over to me. He patted me on the shoulder as he whispered in my ear, "Trust me, son; I won't let you down."

I can't tell you why—I really didn't know this man at all—but suddenly everything was immediately all right. I felt a strange calm inside, very peaceful and well grounded. All he had done was touch me on my shoulder and whisper a sentence in my ear, but somehow I instinctively knew that if Mr. Kane said to trust him, I could.

2

RISE 'N' SHINE

Something was blaring in my brain. I opened my eyes and saw that the clock said 4:00 a.m. I reached over and switched off the alarm. The blaring stopped.

By 4:25 I was standing on the front porch of the Malihini Hale. Then, precisely at 4:30, I saw the headlights of Mr. Kane's cab as it entered the inn's long driveway and drove up to where I was standing. "Good morning, Mr. Langston," Kane said through the open passenger window. "Are you ready to learn the secrets to building the personal wealth and happiness you so desperately seek?"

"Just give me the wealth lesson, and I'll buy all the happiness

I can stand," I replied, instinctively realizing that was not the best reply as a look of sadness came over Mr. Kane's face.

I opened the door, got in, and said, "OK, how do you want to do this?"

Mr. Kane smiled at me and said, "Patience, my friend, patience. Let's go look at the sunrise first. I want to take you to my favorite place, which I call 'Sunrise Mountain.'"

Are you kidding? I only have one day with you to learn every-thing you have learned in a lifetime, and you want to waste time watching the sunrise? That's what raced through my mind, but I managed to say instead, "Whatever you wish, Mr. Kane."

Mr. Kane just nodded to me and smiled.

It took about an hour to drive up to the top of the mountain on the southern part of the island. I couldn't see much because the sky was pitch-black with no moon. One thing I will never forget is the incredible smell of eucalyptus as we drove up the mountainside; it smelled just like the cough drops.

We finally reached the top of the mountain, and Mr. Kane turned the taxi so it faced due east. We then began waiting for the sun to rise. He looked at me and said, "Money is of no value unless you learn to enjoy life first. I start every morning up here, to marvel at the sunrise and give thanks to the Lord for another day. Mr. Langston, when was the last time you began your day watching the sun come up and thanking the Lord for it?"

He had me. About the only time I could remember seeing the sunrise was on a goose-hunting trip one of my friends took me on about ten years earlier. My silence provided Mr. Kane with all the answers he needed.

"You see, Mr. Langston, if you start each day in the presence of such beauty and wonderment, it will do more than just make you excited to be alive. It will also stimulate you to make the best of this day God has given to you." He then became very quiet and focused on the eastern sky.

I decided to follow Mr. Kane's advice and watched the sunrise with him. I paid particular attention to the sounds of the newly awakened birds and even heard a slight breeze as it rustled through the trees. Right before sunrise I noticed the temperature drop a few degrees and smelled the eucalyptus trees again. I had never felt so alive and excited. I said a little prayer and thanked God for making this day a possibility, as I knew it truly was the first day of the rest of my life. I made myself a promise then that I would start every day from there on this way. After all, if it was good enough for Mr. Kane, who was I to argue?

Ten minutes after the sun broke the surface of the ocean, Mr. Kane looked at me and said again, "Money is of no value unless you learn to enjoy life first. Never forget this, Mr. Langston. Most people feel if they could only get enough money, then life would finally be enjoyable, but I can promise you it doesn't work that way. Unfortunately, I had to learn this lesson the hard way." He then paused before asking, "Are you ready for me to tell you my story?"

Without answering, I got my voice recorder ready and switched it on, and he began.

"I was born here on Kiki Loa to a poor farmer and his wife. I was the sixth of what later turned out to be thirteen children. We were incredibly poor. My mother and father both worked fourteen hours a day in the sugarcane fields, just to put food on the table. I started working in the fields when I was twelve.

"I decided when I was thirteen that I would leave this island and become a success. My father just laughed at me and said,

'Akamai, every young boy on Kiki Loa says that when he reaches your age, but no one ever leaves. Learn how to enjoy life, and the work won't seem so bad.'

"'Enjoy life! How could anyone enjoy this type of life?' I would ask him, but he would just laugh and say, 'One day you will learn how.'"

Mr. Kane took another long look at the sun, now seemingly just a couple of feet above the water. He took a deep breath, releasing it with a little sigh of pleasure, and continued.

"When I was fourteen, I had become even more certain I was going to get off this island. I wanted to get a good job making lots of money and become a wealthy man. While I still hadn't figured out how I was going to get off the island, one day I figured out how to get out of the fields.

"The parents of the present owners of the Malihini Hale had just decided to turn their home into an inn. I knew that the work would be more than they could handle by themselves, so I asked them if I could help with their guests. I told them I could help keep the rooms clean, do the laundry, and clean the kitchen after the meals. I even offered to tend the garden. To my surprise, they accepted and offered to pay $2.54 more a day than I was earning in the sugarcane fields.

"My father was both surprised and impressed. He couldn't believe my good fortune. But to his dying day, he never realized that it was my burning desire to leave the fields that created that opportunity for me. It was my never-ending search for a solution to my quest that made me think of and then pursue that job.

"You see, Mr. Langston, my father always thought that my opportunity was created by the owners of the Malihini Hale. But I say that if I had accepted my fate and become resigned to working in the fields for the rest of my life, another boy would have gotten that job. My father—bless his soul—always was waiting for opportunity to knock on his door. I, on the other hand, decided that I would have to create my own opportunity.

"In fact, Mr. Langston, let me share a secret with you. I felt that same type of burning desire in you after reading your letter. All the other letters were too professionally written. They were very slick and expertly conceived, but yours displayed your real passion. I knew that if you could capture that passion in telling my story, you could have a positive effect on millions of people's lives."

I was stunned. I had come so close to sending the other letter.

Noticing the surprised look on my face, Mr. Kane added, "Never be afraid to let your real passion show, Mr. Langston. It will open more doors and enroll more people than wit and intellect ever will."

3

A VISIT FROM MOSES

We had just started back down the mountain, heading for the village. I was amazed at how much I had already learned, and Mr. Kane hadn't even started yet. It was then that I noticed how different everything looked in the light of day. We had just passed this way less than an hour ago, but now I could see the eucalyptus trees I could only smell then. They were so incredibly tall that they almost blocked out the sky. The beauty of this place was overwhelming.

Mr. Kane must have been reading my mind because he said, "Don't be afraid if the truth reveals itself to you and it is not what you were expecting to find. Many people reject truth when it is shown to them because it seems too simple. The truth is very much like this road. You traveled it an hour ago in darkness and saw nothing. Now we are at the same place as then, and look around at all that can be seen when you put a little light on the subject.

"Today, Mr. Langston, I am going to teach you a complete system for creating wealth. I guarantee it will work for you, and for anyone who reads the book you write, if you simply follow this system. But contrary to what you might expect, wealth is not achieved by making great investments or taking your company public. The true development of personal wealth is first achieved in the mind, and anyone can do it.

"The system I will teach you today has many components; each is vital in making the system work. It is imperative that you study each component until you understand why it is important and how it works. It is also imperative that you integrate all these pieces of the system together if you want to produce the maximum results.

"Let me warn you again, Mr. Langston: what you are going to hear today may at times not have anything to do with what you thought you were going to hear. But if you will trust in me, I am confident that by the end of the day you will see how everything we discuss works cohesively together. When combined, it can do nothing other than produce the results you so intently want.

"You see, Mr. Langston, for me it all started while working at the Malihini Hale. It was there that I met the man who was responsible for changing my life. He revealed to me the first real secret I learned of life, but it was the one truth that has enabled me to become all that I have become.

"When I was sixteen, he came and stayed for a while as a guest at the inn. He always seemed eager to chat. His name was Moses. He never told me his first name and insisted I just call him Moses. No *Mister*, no nothing, just Moses. So I did.

"Moses was a phenomenal man. He truly was a modern-day philosopher. I stayed up very late every night as Moses explained to me the way things really work. One night I shared with him my dream to leave the island and get a high-paying job so I could become rich, when Moses turned and looked me right in the eyes and said, 'Akamai, the secret to getting everything you want in life is learning to program your subconscious mind.'

"This was very puzzling to me, as I really didn't understand what he meant. How does one program the area of one's mind that is already in control of every action you make? It truly seemed impossible to me.

"A few nights later, while sitting on the porch of the Malihini Hale, Moses reached into the satchel he always carried and took out a book,[1] which he handed to me. The book was called *I Can*, by Dr. Ben Sweetland. Moses looked at me and said, 'Akamai, this book will answer your question about how to program your subconscious mind. Study it well and you will learn the secrets of obtaining everything you want in life.'

"I was so excited that I immediately excused myself and went to my room to begin reading my new book. By morning I had finished it.

"In this book, Dr. Sweetland discussed the power of the conscious and subconscious (creative) mind. I learned that the

---

1   Ben Sweetland, *I Can: Grow Rich While You Sleep* (n.p.: Wilshire, 1985).

conscious mind is the size of a peanut next to the subconscious mind, which looks like a watermelon by comparison.

"The book pointed out that most people believe that, due to the sheer size of the subconscious mind, it is in total control of the conscious mind and, therefore, of everything we do. Most people believe their subconscious minds control their moods, energy, personal drive, and every conscious thought they have. In retrospect, at this time in my life, I and everyone in my village subscribed to the same theory. If someone were depressed, we just accepted it as a fact, out of one's control to change.

"In reality, through *I Can* and Moses, I have come to understand that just about everything in life works in almost the exact opposite way of what we logically believe. For example, the human mind works exactly in the reverse of how I was taught. The subconscious is not in control of the conscious, but vice versa. The subconscious mind has no will of its own or any conscious thought. Will and conscious thought are reserved solely for the conscious mind. The subconscious mind is like a large, fertile tract of land. If you plant sugarcane seedlings, it has no option, if cared for properly, but to produce a healthy field of sugarcane. Likewise, if you plant something poisonous, like poison ivy, you're going to get that instead.

"Learn to master this concept well, Mr. Langston, and you will have learned to control your destiny. Once mastered, you will literally be able to choose what type of day you're going to have, good or bad, every day for the rest of your life."

With that statement, Mr. Kane pulled the cab into the driveway of a small café named Kalinai Café and got out. "Let's have breakfast, Mr. Langston. I'm starving."

4

WILD FANTASIES

The waitress poured me a cup of coffee. Its aroma seemed to fill the tiny café. Mr. Kane had been watching some birds building a nest in a tree outside the café's front window. He started speaking without looking at me.

"Mr. Langston, the next piece of life's puzzle came into place with my introduction to the remarkable power of goal setting. Once again it was Dr. Sweetland, at Moses' suggestion, who showed me how to master this technology. Most people readily accept the power of setting goals. Life is full of clichés concerning the value of one's setting and achieving goals; however, many people just don't know how to put real shoe leather to this technology and get it to work in their lives.

"One night Moses instructed me to list my wildest financial fantasies on a three-by-five card. He then told me to pull this card out several times a day and daydream about what it would be like to own all those things. At the age of sixteen, this seemed quite natural for me, since much of my life was spent daydreaming about getting off the island anyway.

"Moses told me to pretend that the postman rang the bell on the front door of the inn and gave me a certified letter that stated I had a rich uncle (who I didn't even know existed) who had just left me everything on my list. Next, he told me to visualize myself enjoying each and every one of those things I had just received. He told me to really exaggerate my daydreams and play this game as often as I could remember each day.

"This project was a lot of fun for me. I listed on my three-by-five card that I wanted to go around the world, have a Lincoln Continental with a telephone (a very rare item back then), own a Corvette sports car, have $10,000 in the bank, own a wardrobe of custom-tailored clothes, and live in a five-bedroom home with a swimming pool.

"I wrote my goals down on my three-by-five card exactly as Moses had instructed, and the first day I read and fantasized about them about ten times. The second day I did it about seven or eight times, the third day maybe five or six, and then once or twice a day for maybe another week or two before I lost the card.

"What I didn't realize at the time was that my conscious mind was giving explicit orders to my subconscious mind. After I lost the card, I didn't consciously think much about those goals anymore.

"Looking back, Mr. Langston, I realize today that one of the most important elements in this whole scenario for me was my age. My goals were limitless and were not tempered by whether or not they were possible to achieve. Instead, I possessed that open-mindedness that comes so easily with youth.

"Then one night, Moses began our conversation, 'Akamai, I have something important to tell you. I am leaving Kiki Loa next week and returning to the States.'

"I was devastated! Tears instantly began welling up in my eyes. Moses was leaving, and I would never see him again!

"Then Moses said, 'Akamai, please listen carefully to what I have to say. I think you are a remarkable young man. You remind me a great deal of myself when I was your age. I never had a son; but if I had, I would have wanted him to be just like you.

"'Akamai, what I am saying is, I would like to take you back to the States with me and offer you a job as a salesman in one of my companies. What do you think?'

"I was overwhelmed! I couldn't believe what I was hearing. Moses was offering to take me to the 'promised land,' just like in the Bible.

"The next day I went to speak to my father and asked his permission to go with Moses. I was petrified he would say no, that my place was here on the island with my family. Instead, he said, 'Akamai, I have always known you were a very special child and would grow up to accomplish great things. I knew if anyone would ever leave this island, it would be you. Go, and God bless you, son, for today I am the proudest father in the world.'

"The next week I went back to the States with Moses and began working as a salesman in one of his companies, just like he promised. Within a short period I became one of that company's top salesmen and started earning between $150 and $250 per week, which back in the late '60s was a fortune. The next summer I was promoted to a junior management position and started supervising other salesmen. I began earning $300 to $400 a week.

"One of the other companies Moses owned imported custom-tailored clothes from Hong Kong. One of the tailors from Hong Kong traveled throughout the United States and took measurements of Moses' customers to guarantee a good fit when the clothes arrived. His name was Tommie Cheng. I became very good friends with Tommie and spent extensive time with him every time he came through my city.

"In January of the next year, Tommie and his cousin were getting ready to take a three-month vacation around the world. I told him I had dreamed about traveling around the world, and he invited me to come along. I can remember saying at that time, 'Sure, Tommie, but I am one of Moses' top salesmen; he would never let me go.' So I just envied him and let the thought drop.

"The day before Tommie left for his trip, he repeated his invitation. That day I sat daydreaming at lunch about what it would be like to take that trip and decided to give Moses a call and at least ask. All he could say was no. Boy, was I surprised when he said yes!

"I had enough money saved up to purchase my plane ticket, and Tommie offered to let me stay with him in his rooms and pay for my meals. So within an hour I was home packing and left the next day for three months to take a trip of a lifetime.

"When I returned home, I started back to work in my old job for Moses. My career in his company continued to climb, and by the next summer I had my own three-thousand-square-foot office, complete with secretary and a dozen salespeople.

"That next year I traveled with Moses' company to several of its offices and acted as a troubleshooter. Later that year I moved to St. Louis and opened new offices there. Within a year I was the division manager of the Midwest division, overseeing the company's activities in St. Louis, Kansas City, and Omaha.

"When I was twenty years old, I was moving out of a house I had been living in when I came across an old, crumpled-up, three-by-five card that fell out of a family album I had brought with me from Kiki Loa. I uncrumpled it and, to my surprise, found my original goal list (long since forgotten). *That, Mr. Langston, may have been one of the most riveting moments of my life!*

"Here I was, moving out of a five-thousand-square-foot, six-bedroom house with a pool. I was still single but had two cars, a Lincoln Continental with a telephone and a Corvette. I had a closet full of custom-made clothes made by my friend Tommie and had $10,000 in my savings account. And, as I just told you, I had previously traveled around the world.

"I can remember to this day the exact feeling of elation as I grabbed a new three-by-five card and began selecting new goals. These new goals appeared just as absurd to my current financial picture then as the earlier ones I had written when I was sixteen back on the island of Kiki Loa. I wrote down on the new three-by-five card that I wanted to be a millionaire before the age of twenty-five, be worth $10 million before I was thirty, and have $25 million before age thirty-five. I wrote that I wanted to live in a multi-million-dollar estate on prime acreage and own a Rolls-Royce Corniche convertible and a limousine. I also wanted to own a yacht and a professional football team. Finally, I wanted to have a million dollars in the bank so I never felt poor again.

"Once again, Mr. Langston, these wishes were completely out of my grasp, and I had no plan of action to get them. But I did follow the exercise that had served me so well back on Kiki Loa and began daydreaming all over again.

"Within a year, I assumed the job of national director of marketing. My salary was established at $42,000 a year with stock options.

"Six months later I was visiting Moses at his home in Dallas for Christmas. At dinner one night I began talking to an attorney who was a close friend of Moses. He wanted me to meet one of his clients who was a financial consultant to many wealthy people. During the discussions I realized that Moses' friend was trying to set up a job interview. I thanked him and told him I was very pleased with my current position, felt a tremendous loyalty to Moses, and therefore wasn't interested. Then he said, 'Well, Moses thought you would at least like to meet this guy; he's only twenty-seven years old and is already worth $5 million.' Without missing a beat, I said, 'Please set up the interview.'

"Mr. Langston, that interview went extremely well. The gentleman offered me the position of his apprentice as a financial consultant, with no salary, and a required six-month period of training. The only thing he did offer in the form of compensation was a free apartment in one of the apartment complexes he owned.

"This presented the most difficult decision of my life. I was set; I had a great job and a great future with Moses. But I also knew I was completely naive when it came to money. I felt confident that I would always be able to earn good money, but I also knew nothing about how to make money earn money.

Deep down inside, I had the intense fear that someday I would be fifty years old earning $100,000 a year, have other great cars and travel memories, but have only $25,000 in the bank. To me this job potential was an opportunity to learn the secrets of true personal financial management. And I knew Moses must have arranged that interview for a reason; so I opted for the new position.

"The next six months were the hardest of my life. I read tax journals, real estate reports, life insurance contracts, and every variety of financial material. I was tested regularly on what I read. I was never so thankful my grandmother had taught me to read English well as a child back on Kiki Loa.

"One day my new employer invited me to attend one of his client sessions. It was fantastic! That day I began to learn that the financial rules most of us have been taught to follow lead to financial failure. I learned that most of the golden financial rules I had been taught were incorrect; in fact, they were dead wrong. Saving money for a rainy day in a savings account was no longer a good idea due to the high tax rates on the interest earned and the loss of purchasing power due to inflation. Paying cash and never borrowing under any circumstances, which my father taught me was right, was also wrong for the same reasons. Just about everything that I thought was right was not. Then it dawned on me, Mr. Langston: if everything we were all taught financially was right, then why was there so much financial failure everywhere?

"To demonstrate what I mean, let me share an interesting statistic with you. According to the Social Security Administration, two out of every three Americans over the age of sixty-five depend on their Social Security check as their principal means of support.[1] Mr. Langston, if all the golden financial rules we are all taught were correct, *wouldn't there be more success?*"

Mr. Kane paused to let that bombshell sink in.

---

1   Social Security Fact Sheet 2015, https://www.ssa.gov/news/press/factsheets/basicfact-alt.pdf.

5

$30 MILLION BY THIRTY-FIVE

Mr. Kane ordered a slice of pie and then continued with our interview.

"Mr. Langston, the next several years were like living in fairyland. Rich people paid me handsomely to review their personal financial affairs and to structure programs to help them attain their financial goals. For me, the most valuable experience of all was being able to review all the mistakes they had made prior to their coming to see me. I was allowed to observe hundreds of millions of dollars of their past investments with 20/20 hindsight and see what they had done right, and much more important, what they had done wrong.

"It was at this time that I began separating my clients' successful investment programs from the failures and begin studying them. I didn't know exactly what I was looking for, other than trying to simply identify common denominators present in both the successful investments and the failures.

"My concept was simple. If I could find things that were always present in the failures and not present in the successes (as well as the other way around), I could begin structuring my own investments to contain only the elements I found in the successful group, and none of the ones found in the failures.

"During the four years I worked for the financial consulting firm, I rose from apprentice to senior vice president. I then left to form my own firm, and I began one of the first 'fee-only' financial planning practices in the United States.

"Over the next ten years, I maintained one of the most successful financial planning practices in the nation. In my tenth year of private practice, I decided to retire and stopped accepting any new clients. At that time I was thirty-four.

"Mr. Langston, it is scary to look at what has happened since my goals list was written back at age twenty. At thirty-four, I was then living on three acres of property with ten thousand square feet of improvements (including an indoor racquetball court). The property was appraised at $4 million. I owned a Rolls-Royce Corniche convertible, a Lincoln limousine, a Mercedes 280SL convertible, a Porsche 928, and a four-wheel-drive Jeep Cherokee. Additionally, I owned a seventy-one-foot ocean-sailing yacht with a year-round crew of four persons. I also had $2 million in liquid reserves. My net worth was over $35 million, and the only thing that I had not achieved on my original goal list was to own a professional football team. However, I did have a contract to purchase the USFL Chicago Blitz, and was going to bring it to Dallas when the USFL started to fall apart.

"If you analyze my story, my friend, the point of all this becomes crystal clear. I started with nothing, have only an average IQ, do not have a college education, and have nothing special I can point to except the tools that were so graciously provided by Moses and Dr. Sweetland.

"I truly believe that the real formula of building personal wealth is that we each have control over our creative/subconscious mind, and can direct it to get us what we want through conscious visual commands. It worked too well in my case, over and over again, not to be true.

"All you have to do, Mr. Langston, is realize that your creative mind is your own personal genie inside Aladdin's lamp. Fortunately, however, it will not limit you to only three wishes; you can have as many as you want.

"Most people are busy looking in other places for the secrets to creating wealth, but the real secret is learning to repeatedly visualize your dreams as real goals, and then staying committed to achieving them. If you plant your goals in your creative mind as visual seeds, and then truly believe that they are going to occur, you can obtain anything you want. I like to think about your creative mind as your divine link to God.

"Mr. Langston, I can promise you that what you consciously think and visualize will manifest in your life. However, you don't have to take my word for this; just look at your past life to this point for validation. You need to do nothing more than objectively study your past thoughts and beliefs about yourself, and then look at your current environment to prove this conclusively.

"Ever since you were a child, whatever you thought true

about yourself and dwelled upon has become your reality. What you program into your creative mind as a conscious belief, good or bad, will later be returned.

"If you accept and believe this as strongly as you believe everything else you know to be true, then it will be just as true for you as well. This in turn will give you unlimited power to program your future through conscious directives to your creative mind, instead of falling victim to letting your conscious mind run uncontrolled without any direction or intent.

"Now, Mr. Langston, it is time for us to take a little ride." Mr. Kane pushed his chair back, stood, and began walking to his cab.

Once we were seated in his car, Mr. Kane drove me to an area near the mountain where a small river had pooled into a large pond that I later found out was called Laniahi Lake, and stopped the cab. We got out of the cab and the water was so clear I could see the bottom. The pond was only about five feet deep, and I noticed that there were hundreds of fish that looked like a cross between trout and salmon floating halfway between the surface and the bottom. Upon closer inspection I realized that many of the fish were dying, and some were already lying dead on the bottom.

I looked at Mr. Kane in panic and said, "What's happening here?"

Mr. Kane gazed into the water and replied, "These are Kioana fish, my friend. They are very much like the salmon in British Columbia. These fish fought their way upstream to lay their eggs, and now that the job is done, they are all dying. You see, Mr. Langston, the Kioana accomplish a near-impossible feat by making it to this pool. The trip up the river, according to the scientists, is next to impossible for fish to achieve. At several points, the river becomes so narrow and shallow that the Kioana have to jump on the bank and flop several yards to get to the next pool. Many don't make it.

"The only reason these fish are here in front of you, Mr. Langston, is that their desire was so strong to be here that they accomplished the near impossible. The reason they are dying now is they have achieved their main life's goal and have no remaining goals left to drive them forward.

"This exact same thing happened to me, figuratively speaking. You see, my goals list ended at age thirty-five. That was as far as I had set it at age twenty. By thirty-five, I had everything I ever wanted. There were no cars left to buy. I was already tired of maintaining an extravagant residence. My boat, with all its related mechanical breakdowns and crew changes, became a possession that possessed me. Further, I had not set any new goals for my life. Therefore, I retired from practice and left most of my money invested in prime real estate. Life had become exactly as I had planned.

"Then the unthinkable happened. The U.S. economy hit the skids. The real estate market crashed overnight.

"I spent the next three years of my life trying to protect what I had built. I used up all my liquid reserves trying to service the debt I had against my real estate properties. Then, one by one, I lost my real estate investments and had to sell the cars and boat. Finally, my home itself came into jeopardy.

"It was at this point that I learned the next major lesson of life, Mr. Langston: how to achieve true financial security. I thank God I learned that lesson at the age of thirty-five instead of sixty-five.

"Most people who develop large estates do so through a system of investments. They learn how to do something very well—maybe it's real estate, stocks, or oil—and then they keep learning more and more about their investment area so that they can consistently make more and lose less. It becomes a kind of game. The more you do it, the more it works; the more it works, the more secure you feel; the more secure you feel, the more you do it."

At that moment, Mr. Kane stopped and stared so deep into my eyes that I felt he was seeing directly inside of me. Suddenly he said, "*There is no security in this concept*, Mr. Langston! Investments should be a direct solution to an individual's personal financial problems and goals. Because all investments put your money at risk, there is always a chance that you may lose some or all of your money. Let me explain what I am trying to say.

"Let's say you want to retire at age sixty-five, with the equivalent of what you can buy today for $6,000 a month. Let's also assume you want to send your two children to college for four years each at a cost today of $15,000 per year. So your goals are to build a retirement and education fund. As you will see this afternoon, Mr. Langston, there is an exact structure by which you can accomplish these desired goals. The bottom line is that you will need to invest X number of dollars at Y percent rate of return for Z number of years to build the funds you will need to accomplish these two things. Therefore, this investment equation becomes your specific investment goal.

"But, my friend, if your newspaper were to conduct a person-on-the-street interview and asked people why they make investments, most would answer, 'To make a profit.' In fact, most people in the investment business try to sell people on the need to always keep your money active and growing. While there is nothing wrong with this philosophy, investing purely with the hopes of making a profit is like buying a rudderless boat. It might be perfectly seaworthy and it will not sink, but you cannot direct it to go anywhere you want it to. The longer that rudderless boat floats around at sea, the greater the chances that something could happen that could cause it to sink.

"If you fail to recognize the important 'secret' of never investing anything without first identifying the goals you are investing to solve, you will ultimately begin investing for investment's sake. Why put your money at risk if you have nothing personally important to gain in your life?

"What I am saying is that if you already have enough, allowing for inflation, to meet your true retirement goals and do not want to raise those goals; if you have funded your children's college educational goals; and if you have obtained any and all other financial goals, possibly including funding future generations' retirements, why put your money at risk if you have nothing left you want or need to gain?

"Think about it, Mr. Langston! Have you ever read a story of how someone who was worth $100 million or even $500 million went bankrupt and lost everything? Have you ever wondered, 'What did this person need that he didn't have already that could make it worth putting everything at risk?' In reality, there was nothing left important to gain that he wanted or needed, and the consequence was losing everything.

"When I look back, I can see how easy it is to get caught in this trap. I started making real estate investments early in my career. As my earnings increased, I increased my lifestyle only slightly and invested the rest in real estate. The more I earned, through both investments and my practice, the more my lifestyle increased; but the size of my annual real estate investments also increased in even greater proportion.

"My financial condition grew almost geometrically each year. Year after year things worked perfectly. This continued for almost two decades. It became a system that seemed to work flawlessly. I felt I was truly financially secure for the first time in my life.

"The problem was that I lost sight of my true financial goals. All of my definitive goals were fully achieved at around $15 million. The income from that sum could have supported me and my family in the manner in which I wanted to live, even after adjusting for inflation, for more than two generations. But unfortunately, I kept doing what I knew best to do, *exactly what I did yesterday that worked.*

"What I failed to see is that there are different processes you must go through at different times and junctures in your life. For example, when you have nothing, the first step is setting goals. While your mind is subconsciously pursuing your goals, it will magically develop your system. When you follow your system, you will begin climbing the mountain of your dreams. No matter how tall the mountain you tackle, it has a summit. When you reach it, you better stop climbing, or you will climb down the other side and end up back at the bottom.

"Mr. Langston, hopefully this illustration, along with my own personal story, helps you understand that the second crucial secret of building real financial independence is recognizing that true security means reaching your mountain's summit, stopping, and then erecting a fort at the top. This fort lets you stake out that mountain as yours so you never lose it.

"The process of building a fort in no way resembles mountain climbing. It is a totally different function. For example, had I stopped my real estate investing at $15 million (because that satisfied my true financial needs) and then liquidated my portfolio, putting the $15 million into cash, two things would have happened differently. First, I would *not* have achieved $30 million by age thirty-five. Second, I would then have had about $20 million (more than my true economic goal required) safely sitting in a savings account instead of what was left at the time—which was nothing.

"I feel fortunate to have learned this secret at an early age. Suppose things had continued just as wonderfully until I was sixty-five years old and maybe worth $200 million and then it collapsed. I would probably have few options or the desire to start over again.

"When you set your goals, Mr. Langston, match your real desires to them. Arbitrarily setting goals such as wealth of $10 million or $100 million can be a mistake. And never let some investment salesman tempt you into investing for the sheer sake of making a profit."

Mr. Kane's point made a lot of sense to me. But of greater importance was that I realized he had just shared with me a concept that even some of the wealthiest people on the planet had yet to learn. This was something that could only be learned by someone who had successfully climbed to the top of the mountain, fallen off, and survived to tell about it.

However, instead of just jumping back on another mountain and trying to climb to the top again, like most people, Mr. Kane had stepped back and seen the final piece of the puzzle. That was why, today, he could give me the gift of a second secret:

"Always know your end game, and when it is reached, throw your hands up in victory, walk away, and enjoy your success!"

6

EASY COME, EASY GO

It was at this point in my conversation with Mr. Kane that I heard a beautiful bird call out a few feet from my car window. A few seconds later I heard another one answer with the exact same call from across Laniahi Lake. Within a few minutes it happened again.

"Do you hear that bird up in that tree, Mr. Langston?" Mr. Kane asked.

"Yes," I answered. "What kind of bird is that? It has such a lovely call."

"That is the Kanoue Kaliki bird, and they are very rare on the island," he replied. "That particular Kanoue Kaliki bird was born in this valley. He stays in that same tree almost all the time. He calls out loudly and a few seconds later, the echo returns from the other side of the valley.

"You see, when that bird was a young bird, its parents were killed and there were no other Kanoue Kaliki birds in this immediate area. He would call out loudly and upon hearing his echo, fly to the other side of the valley in search of the *other* bird who answered his call. But after many months of not be able to find the other bird, which always answered back from the other side of the valley, he one day gave up.

"Now he just sits there in that tree and calls, but no longer bothers to go out and search for the respondent. The real tragedy is that occasionally, when a real Kanoue Kaliki bird does fly through and answers its call, our friend here just ignores it because he already knows it not another bird. Unfortunately, Mr. Langston, people can get stuck in this same way anytime they already instantly know something from their past experience and don't consider any other possibilities."

Mr. Kane began walking along a path next to the lake toward the side of a large hill and asked me to follow him. Pretty soon we were at the entrance of a cave. We entered the cave and walked inside down a narrow path that curved several times as the cave grew progressively darker. After a few more turns, we were inside an area that was about the size of a large bedroom. This area was brightly lit from light passing through a large translucent slab overhead of what looked like yellow amber.

"Mr. Langston," said my host, "the next step in building your personal wealth is in this room. Look over there along the wall."

As I looked, I couldn't believe what I was seeing. The whole wall's surface was covered with emeralds protruding like fantastic geodes out of the rock; they were everywhere. These stones were the most exquisite shade of emerald green I had ever seen. A large pile of them at the bottom of one section of the wall looked as though they had simply fallen off the wall. My mind raced as I realized that this must be the source of Mr. Kane's wealth and that it appeared he was going to give me some of it.

"Mr. Langston, is this what you were hoping to find when you came here?" he asked.

"Never in a million years," I answered. "Who would ever believe something like this really existed?"

"Well, Mr. Langston, your eyes don't lie, do they?"

"No sir, they don't."

"Then please be my guest, and take as many of these as you would like, but make sure you get what you want, because we will not be coming back here again."

I didn't want to look greedy, but I guess I couldn't help myself. I started picking up the stones and looking for the largest, brightest, clearest ones I could find and stuffing them into my pockets. I couldn't believe it! I was now instantly very rich, and it had all just been given to me with no strings attached.

As my pants pockets filled, I started stuffing more into my underwear and then filling the inside of my shirt with them. Because my shirt was tucked in, it held many times more than my pockets. All the time I was doing this, I was thinking about all the things I could buy with this and the new life I would be able to live. It was very difficult to contain this extraordinary feeling.

Mr. Kane just stood there looking at me, smiling as he saw my excitement. Finally, when I couldn't get any more stones anywhere on my body, Mr. Kane asked if I had enough. I assured him I had more than I could ever need. He then turned and started to walk out of the cave, with me in tow.

I had to walk very slowly to make sure nothing fell out of my clothing all the way back to where the cab was parked. After we got to the cab, Mr. Kane opened his trunk and said, "Mr. Langston, you can empty your pockets in here to keep everything safe until we get back to the inn."

As I started pulling the stones out of my pockets, I instantly noticed that the first stones that came out were not emerald green at all but instead a medium blue. I grabbed for more in my pocket and pulled those out, and they were blue as well. I opened the buttons on my shirt and let all of the stones I was carrying in there pour out into the truck, and every last one was the same medium blue color.

I was in a state of utter confusion. *How could this be?* I wondered. *These stones were all vivid emerald green when I picked each one up and studied it before selecting it in the cave.* In my bewilderment I looked at Mr. Kane and said, "I don't understand. What happened to my emeralds? These all look just like some form of blue rock crystal or something."

Mr. Kane replied, "You are correct, Mr. Langston. They are indeed blue rock crystal, which is very plentiful on the island."

"But I don't understand," I protested. "These were real emeralds when I put them in my pocket; I know I wasn't imagining that. How is this possible? You tricked me."

"Mr. Langston, I never told you those were emeralds. I just told you that the next step in building your personal wealth was in that room, and as you will soon understand, it was. Your eyes are what told you that those were emerald, and as you pointed out yourself, your eyes never lie, do they?"

"But how could emeralds change into blue crystal?" I said.

"I just don't get it."

Mr. Kane began to explain. "Mr. Langston, the only light source in that cave is a yellow slab of golden amber, and the color blue cannot exist under pure yellow light in a dark cave. The reason you saw these stones as green is the yellow light became the filter through which your eyes processed everything. Even though these crystals are clearly blue, under the yellow light your eyes were fooled and you thought they were green. Then your mind automatically assumed that these were emerald, and away it ran from there, creating a whole new reality for you that you instantly knew was real.

"You see, my people have known about this cave for generations and have named it Fools Cave. We have used this place to teach our young people a very important lesson, which is the same one I wanted to teach you.

"Many people operate much the same way, Mr. Langston. They rely so much on what they already know from their past experiences that they keep responding the same way to similar situations and keep getting similar results.

"The older we grow, the more we understand life. Life becomes much more defined and predictable. Remember back in your early adult years, when you were going to set the world on fire? Today, you probably recognize that as only the captivating dreams of a naive youth.

"If this describes how you feel, Mr. Langston, then you are not alone. Most of us, as we mature, learn from our experiences what is possible and what is not. Through the years we have learned where our real boundaries lie and how to protect ourselves emotionally by staying within them. It is painful not to succeed or to be rejected.

"One of the characteristics of being human is that we record and store our past experiences and then use them to critically evaluate future options. Whenever you make an evaluation or decision about anything, you run a quick mental check from what you have already learned is true or safe.

"As an example, if you are approaching an intersection of two streets in your car and the green light turns yellow and then red, you instantly know to stop because you have learned that a red light means potential danger and that you must stop. This automatic knowing is a good thing, as it allows you to function more easily in a complex world.

"However, it can also hinder you, as it can automatically shut down possible options available to you because you instantly already knew everything you think you need to know. I call this pigeonholing, because as you encounter anything new, your mind immediately assesses it, trying to label it into some category of experience you understand so you can deal with it safely. Until your mind has done this, you are not comfortable because you do not feel in control of the situation. However, in doing this all the time, you start jumping to conclusions quickly and pigeonholing things often without really analyzing them. In other words, you instantly already know what something is without further investigation, just like our friend the Kanoue Kaliki bird in the valley.

"For example, when you meet someone for the first time, you run a quick evaluation of everything you see and hear. One's appearance, mannerisms, speech, eye movement, and everything else run through your mental computer, and you formulate a quick snapshot based on other experiences from which you have already learned.

"Let's say this new person you are just meeting has a nervous eye twitch in his left eye and speaks in the manner of a 'good old boy.' If you once had an employee with a nervous twitch in his left eye who stole from you, and at another time had a business encounter with someone with a 'good old boy' drawl who cheated you, then the encounter with this new person is probably already doomed. Your internal computer, likely without your even knowing it, is already putting up your defenses, and you will immediately begin seeing this new person from a distrustful light through those past filters you have created. The possibility of a fruitful relationship with him never really has a chance because you already know all you need to know.

"Let's further imagine, however, that this person is really an honest and sincere person. Let's also assume that he has a business background like yours but is very wealthy. Let's finally assume that you spent the last few years developing a fantastic business idea that requires only a financial backer to revolutionize your field in business and that this new person you have just met has been looking for a new business in which to invest.

"Unfortunately, you probably will never learn all of this about this person because you already will have assessed him. You already know everything you need to know, and because you believe this person is shifty and probably crooked, you get away from him before you ever really try to communicate with him.

"This illustration has much more impact on our lives than it appears. We always rely on our past to create quick and complete assessments and evaluations. Therefore, we are forcing our future to comply with what we already know from our past. The older we get, the more tomorrow has no choice but to turn out like yesterday. As someone recently put it, Mr. Langston, insanity is doing the same thing over and over and expecting different results.

"Suppose you have become cynical, resigned, or angry about life. Everything that happens to you will be filtered through this attitude. No real opportunities will exist for you because you will kill them off before they can mature. Unfortunately, this same system works in every area of your life, not just in finances or business. It works in family relationships, personal relationships, and everything else important to you.

"Mr. Langston, if you live life from your past critiques and evaluations, *then you have no option but to repeat the past!*"

I then interrupted Mr. Kane and asked, "But how can you correct this problem? It seems like such an inbred trait."

Mr. Kane answered, "Recognize first that this is not your problem alone. Each of us is human and operates the same way. For this reason most of us never truly break through to achieve our real potential. We are too busy listening to a little voice in the back of our heads, telling us what we can or cannot do.

"If you insist on relying on what you think you know as the real truth, then you have condemned yourself to repeat yesterday again tomorrow. Stay open to the possibility that instead of the truth, all you have is *your interpretation* in any situation and that there are many other possible interpretations that could be derived from that same set of observable facts.

"Once I began to live with new perspectives, Mr. Langston, life began to hold new possibilities. My new perspective is simple: I don't have all the answers, and I will try most anything *more* than once. And I can honestly say I cannot wait for ten or twenty years from now to see what new things I have learned by then.

"It is true that each of us, through a natural defense mechanism, has built barriers that protect us from life's potential problems. But these barriers also are boundaries to limit our growth. They create the limiting answers that say, 'You can't do that'; 'It will never work'; or 'Why try? It won't make any difference anyway.' These answers put the lid of 'reasonableness' on any goal you set.

"For example, as I mentioned earlier today, I have twice set detailed goals for my life. The first time I was sixteen years old; the second time I was twenty. The goals I set at twenty ran out at thirty-five. At age thirty-five, I retired not only from my practice, but in a real way from life itself. At age thirty-four, I had a fantastic lifestyle, full of fancy cars, yachts, and an elegant estate. Unfortunately, like the Kioana fish, there was nothing else I wanted.

"Life, from that point, over the next few years, Mr. Langston, was an interesting observation in true diversity. At first it made me angry and antagonistic. Nothing was really good enough or any fun. The waitress at the restaurant didn't provide adequate service. The airline personnel were rude. The yacht wasn't as much fun as it used to be. I began to expect too much!

"Then about three years later, the real estate crash occurred that started wiping out my hard-earned investments, one at a time. I fought aggressively to keep them, using all of my cash reserves over the next several years to save them, and finally, the very foundation of my security—my home, was gone.

"Interestingly, during the stage of my life when I had everything and 'Life is no fun anymore' was my constant refrain; I was always angry and full of criticism. I knew how people should act, and they weren't measuring up. I can remember saying to myself, *If I died in an airplane crash, it would not be a big deal. I have already had a great life and do not feel I have left anything undone.*

"Later on in my 'Everything I've worked for is disappearing' stage, I was agonizing over how painful it would be to lose everything and to start over. I might say something like, *Well, I don't know that it was all worth it; I don't think I want to put out that much effort again.*

"Then I had the scariest period in my life. I call it the 'My God! You're thirty-five years old; you don't have a college education; you haven't held a job working for someone else since you were twenty-three; what are you qualified to do?' stage. I *already knew* that I was unemployable. Either I would be a threat to a personnel manager because of my accomplishments, or I didn't have the education and skills somebody in the 'real' job world would need.

"Then the conversations in my head started. *Why didn't I quit when I was ahead? Why did I live so extravagantly? What are you going to do now, big shot?* I started to wonder if the power-of-positive-thinking stuff had ever really worked at all. Maybe there really was nothing more to my life than being at the right place at the right time.

"One day I realized how natural (and fun) it was to wallow around in self-pity and doubt. It was *so* easy to do. I looked around me and recognized that many of my friends who had also experienced a similar financial fate due to the collapse of our economy were doing the same thing.

"After a few years of doing this, I began to clearly see how powerful the negative seeds I had been planting in my mind were, and what a huge field of poison they had become.

"For me, the transition from negative to positive seed-planting was not easy even after I fully recognized it. I would try being positive for a while and then slip back into my own negative, self-doubting perspective. It was almost like beginning an exercise program when you are badly out of shape. It wasn't happening easily and was actually painful. My whole world had quickly become shaped by the negative perspective I had developed.

"Then one day I just made up my mind: *No more! Enough is enough!* I read *I Can* by Dr. Sweetland again and burned the bridges to the conversations that gave me the option to be complacent and mediocre. I decided that failure, fear, and depression were no longer options in my life.

"I had already learned that to grow a large positive field, you must tell everyone around you what you are privately telling yourself.

"When I slipped into a negative, limiting, self-doubting dialogue with myself, I screamed internally, *Stop that! This is not what you want. Get back on track!*

"Mr. Langston, a truly amazing thing happened when I burned my bridges to the negative conversations about my failure. Because failure was no longer a possibility, everything in my life flip-flopped almost immediately. Without the usual pain of a new exercise program or the discipline required to begin a diet, positive seed-sowing became quite easy and natural. In the few instances when I found that I had slipped off track, it was easy to get back on.

"The main difference between the negative and the positive was simply readjusting my dialogue to say that failure, fear, and depression are no longer what I am about. I am about success, accomplishment, and the happiness and energy that come from being proud of me. These aren't mere words to me, but the very foundation of my existence.

"The great part of all this is that it works. *It really works!* Life turned around almost immediately.

"I was no longer afraid of what might happen if my home were foreclosed, or if my new business I had been developing for two years didn't make it. I was full of the knowledge and belief that everything was okay. I was in control . . . I even picked up a new three-by-five card and created some new goals.

"Then, after a while, I noticed something very interesting occurring I would like to share with you. Things were definitely getting better, but there seemed to be a limitation to it all. Having fallen so far and hit so hard, I was playing it safe. I was projecting in my goals only what I felt I could do. For example, my goals for the next five, ten, or twenty years centered on getting back to where I had been. They were nonspecific and had no fixed time periods. They lacked the youthful fantasy of my previous exercises. They lacked that ridiculous and absurd selection process that paid no mind to whether the goals were probable or possible, whether I could or couldn't.

"This little nuance held major repercussions. By playing it safe, even though I didn't know it, I was still engaged in limiting conversations. I was analyzing and evaluating whether I believed this or that was possible based on my knowledge of life. I was carefully orchestrating life to comply with what I already knew was possible and safe.

"This was not how things worked for me in the beginning, or during my successful years. Back then I had no idea where I was going or how I was going to get there. I simply had planted fantastic, impossible seeds and believed with all my heart that they would produce. And they did.

"The day I finally recognized this was almost as exciting as the day I found that old, crumpled, three-by-five card. I spent several hours outlining my goals in every area of my life. Not just money and business, but family relationships, vacations, health and exercises, charitable work, and so forth.

"At first, I had a difficult time breaking through. I still found myself asking, *Can I really do that by then?* Then I shattered all limiting conversations. I set goals as ridiculous and absurd for the age of forty-five as my goals were for a sixteen-year-old living in a three-bedroom apartment. A mere three-by-five card wasn't nearly large enough. My goals grew to occupy seven pages on a legal pad. And Mr. Langston, as you probably have already realized, all of them have come true."

I thought about everything Mr. Kane had just explained since visiting the pond. It not only made a lot of sense; it was also some of the most profound and deepest thinking I had ever heard. It certainly wasn't the way I thought about things, and I was now only beginning to realize just how much experience this man really had.

Then a sad thought hit me: *Mr. Kane is a special person, and I could never be like him. He simply has the power to make things happen that I don't. When I get depressed, I am not thinking about anything except how bad things are or how bad I feel. All I can do then is wait for it to lift so that things look brighter again.*

Mr. Kane must have noticed the look on my face because he said, "You look a little sad right now, Mr. Langston."

I told him I was and then explained to him what I had been thinking.

"Mr. Langston," he said, "you and I are no different, and I have no special powers. I have just learned to start listening in on the conversation I am having with myself, and if I don't like what is being discussed, I start marking some adjustments.

"So let me ask you, Mr. Langston: does what I have explained make sense to you; and if so, do you believe it?"

"Yes," I answered immediately, "it makes perfect sense."

"Good," Mr. Kane said. "Then let me give you a little tool that can help you learn to do what I do. In order to do this, I want you to do a little exercise with me.

"Please think of a time in the last thirty days before coming here when you were very happy."

I thought for a second and started to smile.

"Have you got it?"

"Yes," I replied.

"OK, then please tell me about it," he said.

"Well, it was when I got your phone call telling me you had selected me to write this book about you. I don't think I will ever forget what that felt like."

"Good, Mr. Langston. Now think about another time in the last thirty days when you were feeling unhappy and pretty down."

I thought for a moment and said, "I have one. Just two weeks ago I got a very bad tooth pain when I drank some cold water, and I just knew I was going to need a root canal. I have feared having a root canal since I turned twenty when my best friend had to get one. He was in so much pain during that process that I have always prayed I would never have to have one myself.

"It was two days before I could see my dentist, and all I could think about while I had to wait was how bad this was going to be. Man, was that a bad two days.

"Fortunately, when I did get to see my dentist, he confirmed my tooth was fine and that I had developed sensitive teeth. All I needed to do was use a special toothpaste for a little while until it got better. I instantly felt better!"

As soon as I finished Mr. Kane said, "Thank you, Mr. Langston. Those are two excellent examples. Now I want you to think about both of those times for a minute more, and as you do, I want you to tell me if anything actually changed in your real life between these two events, both good and bad. In other words, did you still have the same home, car, food on the table, family and friends, bills, etc.?"

As I thought about that, I started to see what he meant. The fact was, nothing in my real life really had changed.

"You see, Mr. Langston," he said, "nothing really had changed in your life; but your life felt vastly different during each of these periods, didn't it? In one period you had a terrific high and life was good. In the other, you suffered a lot of high anxiety and fear; yet in your real life everything was really pretty much the same during both.

"The fact is that when you were having your good days, you still had the same real problems and challenges present in your life, just as when you had the two bad days, all of the good things in your life were still present for you as well. The only difference between these two periods was what you had myopically focused your attention on in your mind.

"You see, Mr. Langston, your present reality becomes what your mind fixates upon. If it is about new, exciting possibilities, you are elated; if it is about fear- or anger-based situations, you suffer. All of this is occurring while in reality, nothing has *really* changed in your *real* world.

"Mr. Langston, please do me a favor. Look straight ahead and tell me what you see."

I did as Mr. Kane asked and said, "I see the trunk of your car with my blue crystals; I see the trees around it, the pond next to the car, and I see the sun in the sky."

"Good Mr. Langston, now turn around and describe to me what you see."

I did as instructed and said, "I see the path back to the cave, the large hill it is in, and the blue sky above it."

"Great," said Mr. Kane. "Now, wasn't the mountain still behind you when you were looking straight ahead, even though you couldn't see it? And when you turned around and looked at the hill, even though you couldn't see my car or the pond, weren't they also still there too?

"You see, Mr. Langston, the mind works in the same way. You have all of the good and bad things stored up there. At any time, you can start dwelling on one thing or another and your reality quickly becomes that. Fortunately, most of the time, we do a pretty good job at balancing our focus between the two.

"However, if we fixate on one thing for very long, our reality quickly becomes that. Therefore, your reality is in fact what you are thinking about at any particular time.

"There is always much more that is happening than what you are currently focusing on. This is just like you only being able to see what was in front of you when you looked that way, even though there was still everything else around you that you could not see.

"Think about it like this: Everything you know about your life is in your mind, which is like a dark closet. At the same time, you also have this big spotlight that you can shine on anything in your mind; and what that spotlight shines on becomes your current reality of the moment. Shift that light onto something else and that quickly becomes your reality of the moment. Nothing really changed in your real world except where you have focused your spotlight.

"If you get what I am trying to explain, you will understand that you have infinitely more power over your reality that you ever dreamed possible. If you just run through life on autopilot, you become the victim of wherever your mind chooses to focus your spotlight, with no conscious input from you. On the other hand, if you really understand this, you can always intentionally change your focus and move the spotlight to something more positive that is also just as real."

Wow, I thought. *This is truly amazing!* because I knew Mr. Kane was absolutely right. I mean, I really got it! But then I had a thought, and I spoke it out loud as I was thinking it.

"Wait a minute. How will I know when I am focusing on something bad, because if I am doing that, I won't be aware I am doing it; and if I am not aware of that at the moment I am doing it, how can I change it?"

"Excellent questions, Mr. Langston," he responded. "You are right. When you are in the heat of a fixation, you won't be consciously aware of it. Nor in the beginning will you have the conscious awareness of your need to move your spotlight from it to something more positive that is equally as real. So let me give you a little tip to help you be more aware of what your mind is dwelling on even when you are not consciously aware of it.

"You know how when you are afraid, angry, or have other negative experiences occurring, your body gets certain unpleasant sensations. For me, my chest gets this uncomfortable tingling inside, or I find myself taking deep breaths trying to relax. Sometimes I find that I am clenching my jaw or have my shoulders scrunched up near my neck.

"This is your body speaking to you, because it is responding to what your mind is focusing on, even when you are not consciously aware of it. Therefore, if you start to pay more attention to your body's unpleasant sensation, you can use this as an alarm that you are focusing on something that is not producing a current pleasant reality for you.

"Once you catch this and start exploring what you were thinking about, you can then physically force your mind to move the spotlight away from what it is on, onto something positive that is equally as true.

"Mr. Langston, if you use this process, you can also analyze your life in every area and put a lid on your limiting dialogues with yourself. This will then let you direct yourself toward being everything you ever dreamed of being and having."

This new concept made a lot of sense to me as well as one that I found quite exciting. As we got back into the cab, I vowed to myself to start working on developing this into a new habit immediately.

7

HOW TO LIMIT YOUR RISK

We left the valley with the Kanoue Kaliki bird and the Kioana fish and started back toward the inn. Mr. Kane left me alone with my thoughts for about five minutes and then said, "The more I have seen different areas of my life, the more it becomes obvious to me that life operates as a science. The scientist's job is to do research to learn the secrets his particular area of science holds.

"I first noticed this in the area of investments, and that is a topic you are going to have to learn a lot about in order to start making your money make money. Each investment area is like a different field of science. Stocks, real estate, oil and gas exploration, land, commodities, each has its own distinct rules.

Early in my career I started observing several very wealthy people to try to determine if there were any common denominators in their methods of operation. One common denominator they all shared was their expertise that was responsible for their wealth. They all had become very good in their chosen fields of interest.

"Most investors readily accept the law of risk versus return. In almost any investment opportunity, risk and reward have a direct correlation. However, many investors don't recognize this as a one-way rule. High return usually does mean high risk, but high risk does not always mean a high opportunity for reward.

"One fair definition of an investment is putting your money down on the table, releasing control of it for some period of time, during which you can either make more or lose some or all of that money. Investing, in reality, is a form of gambling.

"Using this definition, Mr. Langston, the riskiest place you could invest your money is on a roulette table in Las Vegas. Las Vegas fits all the definitive aspects under our investment definition, except maybe for prudence. When you put $10,000 down on red on a roulette wheel, in thirty seconds you will have either $20,000 or zero.

"Now, let me use this absurd illustration to make an important point. I would personally sell everything I own and borrow as much money as my signature would carry. I would then go with you to Las Vegas. I would let you pick any casino and any game in the house for me to play (baccarat, craps, wheel of fortune, blackjack, etc.), because it would make no difference. I would even let you select the particular table on which you wanted me to play. I would do all this and place all the money I own on that table and begin to play if I could do one simple thing first. Now, what do you suppose I want to do, Mr. Langston?"

I thought for a moment and said, "I can't imagine anything you could do that would make it safe enough to risk all that you have, Mr. Kane. What would you do?"

Mr. Kane smiled at me and said, "I simply want to take four steps, and walk from the side of the table designated for the players, to the back of the table, and play as the house.

"Now, why can I risk all that I have and gamble with such assurance? Because in Las Vegas the house is not gambling. They don't wake up each morning and wonder how lucky they will be. The casino removed its risks, because it has scientifically analyzed each game backwards and forwards. It has dissected each component of the game to determine the odds of every potential occurrence. It knows every possibility of everything that can happen.

"With this knowledge it restructures the rules of the game and the betting odds so as to place all those odds in their favor. For example, it pays 10 to 1 if the hard eight hits on the crap table, but the odds of its occurring are only 32 to 1. In other words, for every $10 the casino pays out, it collects $32. The only gambler in Las Vegas is the player who accepts the poor odds and attempts to get in under the wire and get back out before those odds stop him."

This immediately struck me as an ingenious concept! *Limit the risk through knowledge and research and then restructure the game and payoffs so as to produce only positive returns.*

"Mr. Langston, this is exactly what most other knowledgeable investors do. They don't rely on their intelligence, or wit, or even their rational minds to make their investment decisions. They either gain the 'knowledge' personally they need through personal experience and study, or they buy it from an expert.

"Because of this, I have come to view the law of risk versus return to mean the novice investor takes the risk and usually loses his or her money, which at the same time allows the sophisticated, knowledgeable investor to reap the returns.

"Experience gives the 20/20 hindsight needed to see the irrational, invisible side of the investment world, or to put it another way, experience allows us to ask the irrational question invisible to the purely intellectual mind. Real knowledge is the key that makes wealthy investors wealthier and over the long run helps to keep transferring to them the assets of the average novice investor. I found this lesson very important as I entered the investment maze.

"One of the biggest phenomena I witnessed as a financial manager was the high propensity of people who earn high incomes for making bad investments. Early in my career, when I was researching my clients' investment portfolios, I separated the good investments from the bad. The amazing thing was how few investments there were in the good stack. Almost every investment that I saw, year after year, didn't work out. It almost seemed that trying to find a good investment was like trying to net a rare, elusive butterfly here on Kiki Loa. You take a swoop at it, and when you check the net, it is empty.

"It didn't seem to matter whether my clients bought an oil-and-gas deal, real estate program, stocks, bonds, mutual funds, cattle-breeding program, or macadamia orchards; they almost always came up losing. The more I researched, the more puzzled I became.

"Finally it dawned on me what was the problem. All my clients were very successful people. They worked very hard and were very good at what they did. That is why they earned enough money to need my services.

"Once these people earned enough to live comfortably, they knew enough to make investments for their future. But their investments almost always went sour. They assumed that because they were very successful in their individual fields, they could simply transfer their knowledge to their investment analysis and enjoy similar success.

"Unfortunately, it doesn't work that way. Each investment area requires a tremendous amount of knowledge to truly succeed. I like to think of each investment area as being a specific scientific field unto itself.

"If you select any single investment area and approach it as a science, you can significantly reduce your risks. For example, if you decided to invest in real estate, you would be competing with the likes of Donald Trump, Ross Perot, and me. Prior to making your investment, you are going to attempt to evaluate site selections, architectural design, tenant mix, rent projection, financing options, and demographics. Either you are going to do all of this yourself or read the prospectus of someone who has a project for sale and is presenting it to you for decision. It should be obvious that your chances of selecting a high-quality project that can make a profit are not the same as Mr. Trump's, Mr. Perot's, or mine. Why can't you do it as well?

"You simply don't have the years of experience Mr. Trump, Mr. Perot, or I have. We know a lot of hidden questions to ask, ones we have learned from our past experiences (successes and failures) that prevent us from making foolish mistakes.

"You see, Mr. Langston; each investment area is like a minefield. It looks perfectly safe to enter, and you don't know you have a problem until you step on a mine. Only after you have done so do you know what not to do next time.

"There are only two ways to successfully traverse a minefield. The first is through prior experiences that have enabled you to walk now on a safe path. The second is to get down on your hands and knees and take it an inch at a time and pray. If you run in blind, you are going to blow yourself up.

"In the investment world this translates to learning from prior experience and spending years of patient research and study to become an expert in that field before ever investing your first dollar. I believe each investment area is a science that in its purest state of knowledge offers no risk, just total reward. If you had enough years and enough lifetimes, you might be able to figure out all the right questions to ask. The more right questions you know to ask, the more risks you can eliminate.

"For example, Mr. Langston, once I saw a tract of land that appeared to be the perfect real estate investment. It was perfectly configured along the frontage on the service road of a major interstate highway and formed the primary corner of the major crossroad in that county. The parcel was two hundred feet deep (perfect depth for fast-food pad sites) and had fifteen hundred feet of frontage along the interstate freeway service road. There was an exit ramp from the freeway at the beginning of the property, so all exiting traffic drove along the property's entire frontage to the corner intersection.

"The site was presented as having water and sewer lines to the property, and review of the property's survey showed a sewer and water line traversing its frontage. A site inspection further revealed a sewer manhole on the property, plus a fire hydrant. To the average intelligent person with a cursory knowledge of real estate, all the homework had been done and this was an excellent site.

"In reality there were a few problems that were not logical to consider that rendered this property virtually useless in its present state. First, the exit ramp off the freeway was a high-speed exit and the highway department would not allow curb cuts along the service road. It didn't want people trying to slow down off the high-speed exit attempting to cross lanes of traffic to enter a fast-food restaurant. Unfortunately, having only two hundred feet of depth, there was not enough room along the backside of the property to run a road (if you could have afforded to develop one for such a small tract in the first place).

"The water line was there as expected (after all, there was a fire hydrant on the property). However, the line was too small and didn't have enough pressure to service the property. The city didn't have plans to increase the size of the water line for eight to ten more years.

"The sewer line was also there on the property, but it didn't service this property. It was located within a paid easement previously purchased across this property. The line was from one small community (to the east) sending its sewage, under contract, to a different community to the west. This property was located in a community that formed a peninsula-like finger that came between the other two communities. This property itself was not allowed to dump its sewage into this sewer line even though it was on its property. The nearest usable sewer line was almost a mile away, due south, up a hill. Sewage doesn't run uphill.

"The point is simple, Mr. Langston. No matter how intelligent you were in this example, the problems of this property would not have surfaced in a logical evaluation. They could have been found only by asking illogical questions learned through past experience. A savvy real estate person would know to ask those questions, to separate the successful projects from the failures.

"This example only confirms what the real environment is like in any investment area. As I said, each investment area is a science unto itself. It contains its own hidden mines that can be located only by asking illogical questions that can be learned only through past experience or research.

"No wonder so many people lose when they try to invest. They naturally assume that because they are good at medicine, law, accounting, or running a business, their expertise will automatically transfer to the investment area they are evaluating. To become an expert in any field of investment requires as much time and energy as it did for these people to become doctors, lawyers, accountants, or business owners in the first place. The casino in Las Vegas didn't just pick a game of chance and make up the betting odds. It did enormous amounts of statistical research to identify its exposure so it could restructure the rules. Therefore, the main function of becoming a prudent investor is learning what questions to ask and what investment parameters you must have present in your investment structure to succeed.

"This can best be illustrated by looking at someone who wants to invest in investment-grade diamonds. Let's say this person did his homework and learned about investing in investment-grade diamonds. He learned all about the four Cs of diamond investing (carat size, color, clarity, and cut). He learned that only diamonds one carat and larger are considered true investment grade. The color must be between D and H, with the clarity ranging between flawless and no less than VVS2, and all stones must be recently certified by the GIA Laboratories. These basics are covered in most investment diamond books, so next the buyer goes to a diamond broker.

"The problem with selecting a diamond broker as an adviser is that he is also a dealer selling his own inventory. Unfortunately, he has to buy all kinds of diamonds (good and bad) when he gets his diamond inventory from De Beers (the diamond cartel). He doesn't throw away the bad ones and sell only the good ones. He has to sell everything he has to anyone that will buy them.

"But, you might say, you have done your research and you know how to pick the good stones from the bad. You know the four Cs and have outlined your parameters. So let's see.

"One of the most interesting things about diamonds is they are not particularly pretty until they are cut. Nature controlled three of the four Cs (color, clarity, and carat size) 20 million years ago when the diamond was formed. But only man, through the cutting process, can release a diamond's inner beauty. And strangely enough, the best diamond-cutting design, the one that makes the diamond the brightest and most colorful, wastes most of the diamond's original rough material.

"Because diamond cutters pay for the rough stone by weight and sell it as a finished cut stone (by weight), there is a natural tendency to leave as much of the rough in the finished stone as possible. But the prettiest (most valuable) stones waste the most rough material. Therefore, the price has to be adjusted downward if the cutter tries to cheat and leave something on the stone that should have been cut away, which reduces its refractive beauty.

"Now, armed with your four Cs as parameters, you are sitting with your diamond broker. To play it safe, you firmly state, 'I want to buy at least a GIA-certified one-carat, D, flawless, well-cut diamond.' The diamond broker shows you a stone certified as a 1.00 carat, D (color), flawless (clarity) stone. It is exactly what you requested.

"Let's assume you are smart enough to know that most sophisticated diamond investors want to buy stones only at least three to five points over the one-carat size (1.03–1.05) and will discount heavily for a 1.00 exact size. That way, if the stone were to get scratched, it could be repolished and not risk going below the crucial one-carat weight parameter. Therefore, you say, 'No, this won't do. I want at least a 1.03 or bigger!'

"The diamond dealer immediately shows you another stone. This new stone is a 1.03-carat diamond with the exact same qualities previously requested. But the certificate reflects the diamond has a 75 percent table (the percentage of the top surface of the stone to its diameter). Again, you are knowledgeable enough to say, 'No, this isn't good enough, either. I want a table between 58 and 65 percent. Because if a diamond's table is too broad, the stone will not disperse light properly and will be heavily discounted at the time of sale.

"The diamond dealer says, 'Okay, you don't want a 75 percent table. How about this beautiful stone?' This time the stone has everything right, including a 62 percent table, except the certificate denotes the stone has a strong blue fluorescence, also a significant discounting factor.

"This game will go on until you are satisfied with a stone and buy it. It will not be until you try to sell your stone for a profit that you will find out whether you asked enough of the right questions.

"Profits are made on most investments when you buy them, not when you sell. If you bought the right thing at a good price, you will usually do all right. And *remember: never rely on a broker as an adviser."*

"Then how do you go about making good investments?" I asked.

"There are no simple, easy answers," Mr. Kane replied. "The only way to get the right answer is to either become an expert yourself or to hire someone from the field in which you wish to invest.

"Should you decide to select an investment expert, make sure you know a lot about him. How is he compensated? Learn how long he has been doing what he does. Look at the actual track records of the past investments he has made and see how much he actually paid back to his investors, net of his fees. The longer the track record, the better. Don't be fooled into accepting projections of what past programs should do with the sale based on today's values as a substitute. Ask for a lot of referrals, and take the time to check them out.

"Let me tell you a little story, Mr. Langston. Once a wealthy Texas oilman was overheard in a conversation with a friend at the petroleum club in which the friend asked, 'Jack, have you ever had that once-in-a-lifetime oil prospect where you knew it was a sure thing? You know, where the oil was kind of standing in puddles on the ground and you knew you had a winner?'

"'Yep!' answered the oil man, 'I see one of those every now and then.'

"'What did you do with those types of deals?' asked the friend.

"'Well,' came the reply, 'I have some good friends on Wall Street who have been kind of special to me over the years, and I usually give them a call and let them put up the money, and we split the profits.'

"'Jack, what about the kind of deal where everything looks good, like the engineering and seismic and all? You know; the kind of the deal you feel is almost certain to hit?' asked the friend.

"'In those cases I usually call my personal banker over here in town. He's been real good to me, and as a favor, I let him put up the money, and we drill the property and split the proceeds,' answered the oilman.

"The friend said, 'Well then, let's go to the other end of the spectrum. Do you ever have a property where the lease is going to expire in a month or two, where the engineering's not too hot, but you have a rig sitting idle nearby, not making any money?'

"The oilman just laughed and said, 'Oh yeah, all the time.'

"'What do you do with them?' asked the friend.

"'Oh,' said the oilman 'I got a bunch of doctors and lawyers who like to say they're my buddy. I just give them a call and let them put up the money. If we find anything, we split the deal.'

"There is a lot of truth in this story. Just choosing a wealthy, successful person with whom to invest is not good enough. Look at his track record very carefully and see how *all* the investors have done over the years. The same is doubly true concerning major investment firms.

"Remember that investing is a science. The more you learn, the more risk you can remove as you learn to ask the right questions. Rarely does someone get rich by accident. And on the rare occasion when that does happen, that someone usually loses it all again through future bad investments. Don't blindly play your instincts based on knowledge from another field. That is the surest way to lose that there is."

8

MONEY WON'T BUY
YOU HAPPINESS

It was around noon when we reached the Malihini Hale. Mr. Kane parked the cab out front and said, "Earlier I told you how to set unlimited goals and follow specific exercises to achieve them. One real challenge is how you will handle life if you should end up getting all the things you have dreamed about for so long.

"Mr. Langston, have you ever read about a famous movie star committing suicide or a super-successful physician getting hooked on drugs, and said to yourself, 'What a waste!' Have you wondered why someone who had it all let it go up in smoke?"

"Sure," I said, "Look at John Belushi, Jimi Hendrix, and Whitney Houston."

Mr. Kane took a deep breath and said, "Mr. Langston, getting everything you want presents a real danger. In our daydreams, when we are sailing on that yacht or driving that fancy car, we feel fantastic and are having the time of our lives. When we daydream and see ourselves experiencing something we really want, we always associate that with feeling good.

"There is an old saying that money won't buy you happiness. I know that this is true. One of the most miserable periods of my life came when I was at the end of my building process and had everything. There was nothing left I wanted to buy, and that was the most volatile situation I have ever experienced. Life had lost a lot of its meaning.

"Now, if you're thinking, 'Yeah, Mr. Kane, I know, but just give me a few million and I'll show you how to do it,' then let's try a little experiment. You are married, Mr. Langston, aren't you?" he asked.

I nodded.

"Good," he continued. "Suppose you and your wife just won a one-month all-expense-paid trip to Europe, with $25,000 a day spending allowance, all tax-free. You and she arrive in Europe with $750,000 to spend. But something happens at the airport, and you get into the worst fight of your lives. You both say horrendous things, and by the time you reach the hotel, you won't say another word to each other.

"By nightfall you still haven't spoken, and all night in bed you are extra careful not to accidentally touch one another for fear the other might mistake this for trying to concede guilt and for an effort to make up. The next day all you hear is this screaming little voice in your head telling you how your spouse has ruined the most important vacation of your life. This gets worse each day for the remaining twenty-nine days left. How much fun would this vacation be?"

"Not very," I answered. "It would probably be the most miserable experience of my life!"

"What about all the money, Mr. Langston? *Money won't buy happiness if you are not already happy.* If you are unhappy and fantasizing about how happy you would be if only you had this or that, stop it! It just doesn't work that way.

"You see, money is a boundary in life. In fact, to adults, it's one of life's biggest boundaries. It defines who you are in society. It tells you what you can and cannot have or what you can or cannot do. It is a structure that governs your very existence.

"I have heard many psychologists say that if a child is not provided with clear, definitive boundaries of what he is or is not allowed to do, he will grow up confused and maladjusted. A child actually finds security in knowing exactly where the limits are so he can function within them. If he crosses the line and is promptly reprimanded, he can then jump back again and things are once again comfortable.

"Most of us have learned to live within boundaries—first at home set by our parents, then at school set by our teachers. Later in life it is usually a job and a boss who set the boundaries.

"Money is also a definitive boundary. If you make $75,000 a year, it sets the limit of what you can do. It says what type of car, what size home, what quality clothes you can enjoy. If you're like most people, you quickly learn to live within this boundary. If suddenly you get a $15,000 a year raise, within a year or two you probably will be living at the limit of $90,000 per year.

"Mr. Langston, I used to teach financial management to graduating seniors at Southwestern Medical School. Quite often a student would become a client a few years later. The transformation from the first year in medical practice to the fourth or fifth year never ceased to amaze me.

"I remember young doctors who had just started practice. They would say, 'As a student, I've been living hand to mouth for the last six years, and I can't believe I'm going to earn $125,000 my first year. I've dreamed about having this much money for so long.'

"In the second year their income goes to $150,000, and shortly thereafter, their lifestyle expands proportionately. The third year they are making $200,000; the fourth, $250,000; and the fifth, $325,000. By the sixth year they can't live on $200,000 a year.

"What happened? As their income increased, they quickly learned to live within the boundaries of their money. In fact, my research on money and lifestyle over the years shows that couples who earn $95,000 a year in this country enjoy the same basic lifestyle as ones who earn $250,000."

"No way," I said. "At least not for where I come from."

"You don't believe so?" Mr. Kane shifted forward in his chair, "Let's see. A person who earns $95,000 a year drives a car equipped with cruise control, an AM/FM stereo with a CD player, power windows, power door locks, automatic trunk release, tilt wheel, and climate-controlled air conditioning. His car is a fully equipped $25,000 Ford. The person who makes $250,000 a year drives a similar car with exactly the same options, but it has a star within a circle as a hood ornament. It is a $75,000 Mercedes-Benz. Now multiply this difference by two cars.

"Both couples dress nicely. At a cocktail party you will notice that the $95,000-a-year couple are dressed, him in a $225 suit, and her in a $200 cocktail dress. The other couple is also there, but the man's suit is an Italian import that cost $1,200, and the woman's dress is made by a named designer and cost $2,500. To observers in the room, they both make stunning couples. Multiply this difference by two wardrobes.

"Both these couples live similarly in their homes. Both have kitchens with all the modern conveniences, but the $250,000-a-year couple's breakfast room is four feet longer and two feet wider than the other couple's. They both have nice master bedrooms that accommodate a king-size bed, two nightstands, and a dresser. But one is thirteen by fifteen feet while the other is sixteen by twenty feet. In the master bathroom one has a sunken man-made marble tub that cost $1,000, the other a Venetian marble tub that cost $9,000. One home has twenty-seven hundred square feet of space and costs $275,000; the other is six thousand square feet in size and costs $900,000.

"When is enough, enough, Mr. Langston? I can remember when my wife and I moved into the new home of our dreams. The living room was thirty by fifty feet. It was a couple of hundred feet from our bedroom to our children's bedroom. We felt lost. Within a week we were afraid that we had made a mistake, that it was too big to be comfortable. Within a couple of years, it wasn't big enough, so we added on.

"Money is indeed a boundary! But what would happen if someone suddenly removes that boundary from your life. Mr. Langston? What if all of a sudden you can spend whatever you want, with no limits? This can be very dangerous!

"I have seen several people I know, including my wife and myself, who suddenly found themselves without monetary boundaries. They made a fortune very quickly and could buy anything they ever wanted.

"As much of a dream as this sounds; it can quickly turn into a full-fledged nightmare. Boundaries create security. You can push hard against the walls, and they are strong and won't yield. This creates a kind of safe zone that says, 'It's all right to bounce around in here.'

"When the walls do come tumbling down, it's sheer excitement. You can buy this and get that. But pretty soon it becomes a test. How far can you go before you *have* to stop? What happens if you don't reach that point? You might decide to reverse directions and run another way trying to find the safety of a nice firm wall. But when there are truly no limits and you can have all the clothes, cars, home, and travel you want, then you begin to think, 'What's next?'

"The most dangerous part, Mr. Langston, is that when you were driving in your Rolls-Royce in your daydream, you were ecstatic. But now, when this is happening for real, after the initial excitement wears off, it is just a car. Your jewelry was supposed to make you sparkle like the diamonds, but you don't. Then a little voice inside you starts saying:

You have everything you've ever dreamed of and you are still not happy.

What is wrong with you?

You're just never satisfied.

Boy, are you a mess; anybody would be thrilled to have everything you own.

"From this unhappiness you grow little seeds of discontent and disgust into a huge negative field in which to live. No doubt some of the *success* suicides and drug addictions we hear about are an outgrowth of this exact problem. In your dreams all you needed was money to buy your happiness; but then it didn't.

"Mr. Langston, if you are not happy with yourself, more money will only make it worse. Don't forget that being a success with your family, friends, charities, church, and community is what it is really all about. "Please promise me that if you use the tools I am giving to you today, you will also focus on these nonmonetary-type goals as well."

9

THE GOLDEN RULE TO FINANCIAL MANAGEMENT

We ate lunch on the back porch of the Malihini Hale. Two peacocks strutted gracefully across the lawn as the waiter delivered our soup. Mr. Kane had grown very quiet for the last ten minutes, and I let him think.

About the middle of lunch, he look up at me and said, "Mr. Langston, my clients all had high incomes and paid high fees for me to manage their financial affairs. Their chances of a comfortable retirement, or any true form of financial independence, before they came to see me, were exactly the same as yours. Successful financial planning has little to do with the amount of income you enjoy, but rather with the way you put that income to use.

"Making vast amounts of money is simply a result of understanding the rules that govern your personal economic environment. Unfortunately, most people in the United States will fail to retire with enough assets to last throughout their lifetime. This probably means that almost everyone you know will end up failing to attain the most basic of economic goals—a secure retirement. Unfortunately, this may include the very people upon whose advice you rely to create your own financial plan.

"The concepts of personal financial management I am sharing with you today may sound simple—in fact, too simple. But don't let this fool you.

"Financial management means that one is directing a flow of events toward predetermined objectives. It means that one is controlling his future financial environment, which may be ever changing, rather than reacting to it. This will require sound planning and precise execution, as well as understanding that true financial management, like other areas in life, is a science.

"Financial management itself is a science interwoven with several other basic sciences. Mr. Langston, your understanding of these other sciences from school will enable you to readily accept and understand the science of money management.

"I have had the very fortunate experience of working with approximately one thousand high-income clients in my career. I have explored the financial history of each to find out what they had done right and where they had erred. I've seen the end result of more than $300 million invested by my clients prior to their coming to me, and most of this money, as I have already mentioned, was lost. It is through these varying sets of circumstances that we will piece together the common denominators of both success and failure throughout the remainder of our afternoon together.

"Mr. Langston, why did you really want to write this book so badly?"

I thought about it for a minute and answered, "Because I was hoping that maybe you would teach me the real secret to building wealth. You know, like the one main golden rule to personal finance."

"Well, my friend," Mr. Kane replied, "If that's what you want to know, let me tell that to you now.

"This is the single most important golden rule you can learn. You might even say that it is the only golden rule of finance you will really need to know."

All of a sudden my heart began to beat faster and my palms began to sweat. This was it. Mr. Kane was going to give me the real secret.

He paused and stared at me intently. Then he said, "The real golden rule of personal financial management, Mr. Langston, is that there *are* no golden rules. *There is no set philosophy or rule that is always right.*

"Yet most people act like there are. They have preset rules they have learned from somewhere from which they make all the important financial decisions of all of their lives. The economy is on an ever-shifting roller-coaster ride, which makes it impossible for any rule to be right all the time. What was right financially in 1950 was, in fact, wrong in 1975. What was right in 1990 was wrong in 2010. And what is right today may be wrong in ten years. Your personal economics change, as do national and international economics; so your concept of what is right or wrong must be flexible to change with them.

"The safest position for you to take is, *do what is right today, with an eye on the future and enough flexibility to change.*

"Recognize that fixed ideas like 'Always pay cash; never borrow' or 'Take a short-term loan with lower interest rates' were right once, wrong at other times, and then right again. Throw away all formal rules about what is right financially, because a fixed line of thought with no flexibility can yield you only a narrow range of growth when you are right and a loss when you are wrong. Flexibility can provide an optimizing factor that will maximize the right decisions and minimize the effects of a wrong decision.

"Making a high income does not guarantee financial success, Mr. Langston. As you personally already found out, it becomes more difficult to stay on top of things financially as your income increases. For many people, making more money is nothing more than obtaining a bigger shovel with which to dig a bigger hole.

"In working with my clients, I had the opportunity to see what they did right and what they did wrong. One of the most obvious conclusions I can draw between the differences in their financial successes and financial failures is the amount of planning they undertook.

"The science of personal financial management is as real as the science of medicine. Certain laws must be obeyed or certain failures become absolutely predictable.

"Take a moment, Mr. Langston, and think about your biggest financial obstacle. What is it?"

I didn't have to think very long on that one. "It's my income taxes; they kill me."

Mr. Kane smiled and said, "While income taxes are a significant problem, the most formidable obstacle we all must overcome in our planning is inflation."

"What?" I said loudly. "You must be kidding. Aren't you a little out of date? Inflation used to be a problem, but isn't anymore . . . right?"

Mr. Kane repeated, "Inflation, for most of the last half century, and especially today, is still the biggest force you must hurdle; and in the near future it might be much worse due to your government's money-printing policies. Unfortunately, many people have simply stopped worrying about inflation because the current inflation rates are reportedly low.

"To truly understand the magnitude of the real problem, we will have to first agree on a definition of inflation. What is inflation, Mr. Langston?"

I thought about that question and remembered back to my single course on economics in college and said, "Inflation is when the supply of a product doesn't keep up with the demand, and as a result the price naturally goes up. That's inflation."

"Not really," Mr. Kane corrected. "The real definition of inflation is: '*an increase in the supply of money without a corresponding increase in goods or services on which to spend that money.*'

"For example, suppose we have a group of fifty hungry people in a room, each of whom has exactly one dollar, and none of them can pool their money. If a person walked into the room with one hamburger, the maximum price for which his hamburger could sell is one dollar.

"At this point you have the theory of supply and demand stretched to its tightest limit. There are fifty hungry people, one hamburger, and yet there is also a limited supply of money. Therefore, even though the supply is limited, the demand critical, the price of the hamburger cannot rise above the limited purchasing power of any single individual.

"Now let's further assume that Uncle Sam walks into the room just before the man with the hamburger and takes each person's dollar bill, tears it in half, recertifies it, and tells the hungry people that now they each have two dollars. Now when the man with the hamburger enters the room, what can they pay for the hamburger? Obviously, the price of the hamburger is now two dollars because the supply of money increased without a corresponding increase in goods or services.

"Because everyone trusts your government and accepts its currency, the price of everything must go up as the government adds more of it to the monetary supply without a corresponding increase of goods and services on which to spend it. Therefore, as I just said, *inflation is an increase in the supply of money without a corresponding increase in goods or services (or hamburgers) on which to spend that money.*

"Is the United States going to have a higher inflation in the future than it has in the last twenty years? To answer that question let's look at the historical debt figures of your country since 1969.

"In 1969 the federal debt stood at $354 billion. It took another seventeen years, until 1986, for the debt to cross the $2 trillion mark. In 1992 it crossed the $4 trillion mark, and then in 2002 it crossed $6 trillion. Now look what happened from then until 2014; the debt grew from $6 trillion to over $17 trillion, with a full 65 percent of that growth occurring just from 2006 to 2014.[1]

---

1   Kimberly Amadeo, "U.S. Economy: National Debt by Year Compared to GDP and Major Events: U.S. Debt by Year Since 1929," *The Balance*, updated September 17, 2016, https://www.thebalance.com/national-debt-by-year-compared-to-gdp-and-major-events-3306287.

FEDERAL DEBT

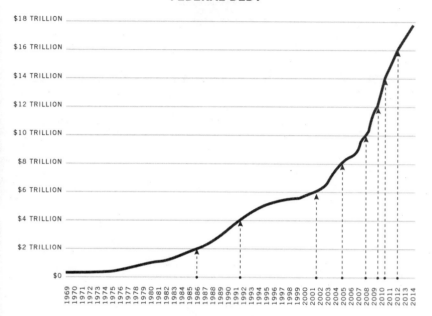

Source: US Department of the Treasury Bureau of the Public Debt

"There are only two ways a country can spend more than it earns. The first is to borrow it, and the second is to print it. Both methods ultimately produce inflation.

"With your federal debt doubling from $8 trillion to $16 trillion in just seven years, that is a compounded growth rate of over 10 percent. So I feel an estimate of 8 percent inflation is a fairly conservative assumption for prudent future planning.

"Therefore, let's look at the long-range effects of inflation over time. Mr. Langston, in this next illustration I am going to assume an 8 percent inflation rate."

With that, Mr. Kane took a paper napkin from the table and carefully drew a chart that looked like this one:

IMPACT OF INFLATION – BASED ON 8% ANNUAL INCREASE

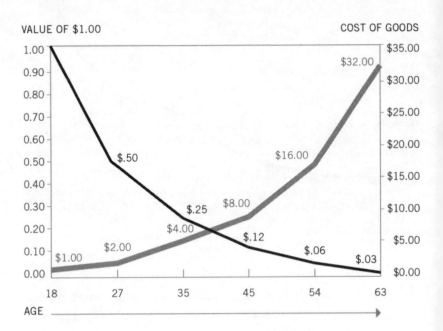

He said as he drew, "Let's suppose a young person is given $1 on his eighteenth birthday; that $1 is being shown as the line that begins at the bottom left corner of this chart. At this time, the value of that $1 is 100 percent of whatever the young person can buy in that present economy, so let's show the value starting in the top left corner of the chart as $1. By the time this person reaches age twenty-seven, the price of the same item has risen to $2, and the value of the original dollar he had at age eighteen has dropped to $0.50 cents. By the age of thirty-six, $4 is needed to purchase the same goods or services. At age forty-five, it's up to $8, at age fifty-four it takes $16, and by age sixty-three (around the age of retirement) it will take him $32 to purchase the same item he used to be able to buy with $1 at age eighteen. The $1 will have shrunk to a value of $0.0313.

"When you view the long-term effects of inflation in this format, it's staggering! But Mr. Langston, this example is not just my projection of the future; it is also a mirror of the past of the last time inflation got out of control in your country between 1969 and 1989.

"In 1969 it cost only $0.50 to go to the movies. And a candy bar or a scoop of ice cream was only a nickel and a dime respectively. In 1989, it cost $5.50 to go to the movies, the candy bar cost $0.45, and the scoop of ice cream $1.

"Now, a minute ago you said inflation was a thing of the past and it hadn't been very high for a long time. Like you, I had been hearing this same thing for the last couple of decades. Yet when I look at the real cost of living compared to what your government was stating as the consumer price index (CPI), I couldn't make it reconcile with the facts I was seeing."

Mr. Kane took out a sheet of paper from a manila folder he had brought in with him and passed it to me to look at. It looked like this:

AVERAGE ANNUAL CPI FOR 20 YEARS	2.495%
YEAR	CPI
1994	2.60%
1995	2.80%
1996	2.90%
1997	2.30%
1998	1.60%
1999	2.20%
2000	3.40%
2001	2.80%
2002	1.60%
2003	2.30%
2004	2.70%
2005	3.40%
2006	3.20%
2007	2.90%
2008	3.80%
2009	−0.40%
2010	1.60%
2011	3.20%
2012	2.10%
2013	1.50%
2014	1.40%

Source: US Department of Labor Statistics

"Mr. Langston," he said, "if you look at the published CPI by the U.S. Department of Labor, Bureau of Labor Statistics, from the years 1994 through 2014, you will see that it has averaged 2.5 percent per year over this twenty-year period.

"Let's look what an actual 2.5 percent per year inflation over the last two decades would look like in reality. A 2.5 percent per year inflation would mean it would take 28.8 years for the price of everything to double in cost, which is an annual increase that is almost unperceivable. That would mean, for quite some time, the price of your groceries, utilities, cars, homes, medical care, and insurance should have been growing so slowly you could not see any significant difference from year to year. Was it that way for you, Mr. Langston?"

"Well, of course not," I said. "Almost everything I have to buy keeps going up in cost year after year. And I can promise you it's a lot more than at an imperceptible rate. Oh, there are a few things that haven't gone up, like maybe computers, home electronics, or a few high-tech items like that, but everything else on which I spend most of my money has gone up a bunch."

"How can the CPI be different from the real inflation?" Mr. Kane asked. "The answer is that the CPI is a composite of certain items people spend money on. Your government chooses which items it wants to use in the composite and what weights it wants to give each item in the average. The CPI also directly has one of the most significant impacts on the annual federal budget of any single factor. For example, Social Security benefits are indexed to the CPI and so are federal retirement benefits. Many parts of your income tax structure are also indexed to it. What this means is that if the CPI is 3 percent this year instead of 1 percent, then the increased cost of Social Security benefits due to indexing would be three times greater. Obviously, your government has a much more vested reason to see the CPI compiled rate come in as low as possible.

"Let me show you what the real inflation has been in your country during the twenty-year period I mentioned earlier, between 1969 and 1989, when inflation was not as tame as it has been since then. I think you will find the impact of this rather startling.

"Let's start by looking at the actual price increases of everyday things that you do or buy." Mr. Kane pulled out three pieces of paper from his folder. The three charts were displayed over the next few pages. The first chart revealed the changing prices of groceries.

Mr. Kane began explaining. "Because everyone has to buy groceries, my foundation solicited the help of a national food chain for this research. The chain's advertising department was contacted and asked if it could locate a newspaper ad it ran in 1969. The young lady helping us found a full-page Sunday ad from May 1969. She picked items from the 1969 ad that would be purchased in our present-day shopping—paper products, meats, processed foods, ice cream, and so forth. She selected only those products that were still on the store's shelf in 1989, when we conducted this research, under the same manufactured name and in the same size package. Here are the results of her selections:

"The first item was Tater Tots. They represent a processed food. In 1969 a bag of Tater Tots cost $0.29 while in 1989 it cost $1.69. That's a 9.2 percent compounded annual increase each and every year from 1969 to 1989. The next item was four rolls of toilet paper, a paper product. Four rolls cost $0.33 in 1969 and $1.45 in 1989. That's an annual increase of 7.7

A COMPARATIVE ANALYSIS OF LIVING EXPENSES

GROCERIES	1969	1989	INFLATION
TATER TOTS	.29	1.69	9.2%
TOILET PAPER (4)	.33	1.45	7.7%
HOT DOGS (LB.)	.69	2.09	5.7%
COFFEE (LB.)	.69	3.05	7.7%
ICE CREAM	.46	2.79	9.1%
SUGAR 5LBS.	.49	2.15	7.7%

percent. A one-pound package of hot dogs went from $0.69 to $2.09, which is an increase of 5.7 percent. Interestingly enough, there were three other meat products in that ad: hamburger, chicken fryers, and chuck roast. Each went up exactly 5.7 percent. So it seems as if *something* had been creating a form of universal control over meat prices.

"The next item was a half gallon of ice cream, which went from $0.46 to $2.79, a 9.1 percent increase. A five-pound bag of sugar went from $0.49 to $2.15, and a one-pound can of coffee rose from $0.69 to $3.05; both show 7.7 percent increase inflation.

"Looking down the right-hand column of this chart, you can see the real inflation that occurred at the supermarket during this period."

A COMPARATIVE ANALYSIS OF LIVING EXPENSES

ENTERTAINMENT	1969	1989	INFLATION
MOVIE TICKET	.50	5.50	12.7%
POP CORN	.10	1.50	14.5%
CANDY BAR	.05	0.45	11.6%
SOFT DRINK	.10	0.50	8.3%
ICE CREAM	.10	1.00	12.2%
HAMBURGER	.35	1.85	8.7%

Mr. Kane looked at the second chart and said, "This chart reveals the rising costs in entertainment. As referenced a minute ago, movie tickets went from $0.50 in 1969 to $5.50 in 1989; and what do they cost today? That is a 12.7 percent increase per year. Now look at what popcorn cost in 1969. It cost $0.10 and you got a bucketful; but in 1989 it cost $1.50 for a little bag, a 14.5 percent increase, and for a lot less popcorn. Again, how much is popcorn today at the movie theater?

"I remember buying a bottle of Coca-Cola for a dime. In 1989 it was $0.50 in the same machine, which is an increase of 8.3 percent. Today it costs a minimum of $1.25 and quite often $2 or more. Again, candy bars in 1969 were $0.05. By 1989, a much smaller version of the same item cost $0.45, reflecting an inflation rate of 11.6 percent, not counting the drop in quantity. A scoop of ice cream went from $0.10 to $1 (now it's upward of $3, depending on the store), and a hamburger went from $0.35 to $1.85. Once again, look down the right-hand column of the chart, Mr. Langston."

A COMPARATIVE ANALYSIS OF LIVING EXPENSES

MISC. ITEMS	1969	1989	INFLATION
SHOES	15.00	75.00	8.4%
SUIT	49.00	250.00	8.5%
DRESS SHIRT	7.00	35.00	7.6%
GAS	.20	1.05	8.6%
SHOP LABOR	7.50	40.00	8.7%
CAR (LUXURY)	4000	20000	8.4%

Mr. Kane then pointed at the last chart and said, "This chart looks at the cost increases in clothing and other necessities. Gasoline went from $0.20 a gallon to $1.05. I can remember buying gas in 1969 for $0.16 at the cheap gas stations. In 1989 it was $1.05, and this was in the middle of an energy glut! In 1969 a fully loaded, full-size car equipped with electric windows, electric door locks, cruise control, and AM/FM stereo cost $4,000. In 1989 a comparably equipped car cost $20,000. Today they are closer to $40,000.

"The point of all of this is simple, Mr. Langston. Many feel that both the CPI and real inflation for the last ten years has been held extremely low as a result of some excellent planning and manipulations by your government's central bank. Those same people are concerned that it will be very difficult to continue to achieve those same results in the next decade. If things during the next twenty years only look similar to those of the past decades from 1969 to 1989, you would have to consider an 8 percent inflation factor a very real possibility.

"When dealing with inflation, you must work with large, unrealistic numbers. Inflation can easily destroy, in a very short period of time, a lifetime of accumulated earnings.

"For this reason, and because in the last several decades we have not seen a constant level of inflation, I suggest you use a long-range inflation projection range of somewhere between a minimum of 5 percent to 8 percent depending on how you feel about what I just explained to you.

"Now in spite of all of this, inflation is not necessarily your enemy. Once you understand it, you can actually harness its power and make it your friend. For example, if you live in a $250,000 house, Mr. Langston, in nine years you will be living in a $500,000 house and you will not have had to move.

"Inflation runs in definitive cycles. These cycles are very long and occur somewhat predictably. They are not like the Dow Jones stock averages, which jump up or down daily at the drop of a hat.

"If you become a student of inflation, you can begin to see these cycles developing. For example, inflation grew steadily from 1969 through 1974, climbing past 12 percent; then it fell off dramatically during the recession that began in 1975. It stayed fairly low during the next couple of years until it began to go up again, peaking out in 1981.

"There are certain investment areas that have a proven history of performing well because of inflation. Real estate is one such area. There also are investment areas that have a history of performing poorly during rising inflation—bond, for example. There are also many other investment areas with a history of doing either well or poorly during periods of falling or rising inflation.

"What if you became a serious student of inflation cycles, Mr. Langston, and when you saw inflation start climbing, you positioned your assets in areas that had a proven history of doing well during rising inflation? Then when you saw the trend reverse and inflation start falling off again dramatically, you repositioned your assets in areas that performed well during periods of falling inflation? Do you think you would end up any better off twenty or thirty years from now than if you just ignored this whole mess and let inflation do to your assets whatever it's going to do?"

It all made a lot of sense. Why be a victim of the system? Why not instead become proactive and use whatever is occurring to my advantage?

One thing was becoming very clear to me in listening to Mr. Kane. There really was a system, and up to this point in my life, I had been oblivious to many of the factors that control the game.

Mr. Kane then said, "Let me share with you a special formula to help you plan for your future needs. It is called the rule of 72. I have already used this formula in my earlier examples of how long it would take for things to double in cost due to inflation.

"If you divide the number 72 by the yield, or growth rate, of any investment, the answer is the number of years it will take for that investment to double in value. For example, if your investment account is earning 6 percent, and you divide the number 72 by 6, the answer is 12, which tells you that a 6 percent investment account will double in value in 12 years. It is that simple. An 8 percent yield on investment means that investment will double in nine years; a 9 percent yield means it will double in eight years; a 10 percent yield will double in

7.2 years; and 12 percent will double in 6.

"Inflation is the same as investment growth, only in reverse, because inflation is actually negative yield. Therefore, instead of making your money double, inflation decreases its purchasing power by one-half. However, the rule of 72 still applies in calculating inflation. Simply divide the inflation rate into the number 72, and the answer is the number of years it will take to make your money shrink to one-half of its current value.

"Now, let's look at what inflation can do to your assets by looking at an interest-bearing investment as an example." As Mr. Kane spoke, he flipped the napkin over and began drawing the following chart as he explained.

ORIGINAL DEPOSIT	$10,000
ANNUAL INTEREST (6%)	$600
TAXES ON INTEREST (28%)	$-168
INFLATION DEPRECIATION (8%)	$-800
BALANCE	$9,632
LOSS	$368

"Looking down the road just a few years, say you had a $10,000 interest-bearing investment for one year that earned 6 percent. Based on a medium tax rate of 28 percent on the $600 of interest, you would have to pay $168 in taxes. And to earn that interest, you had to tie up your money for one year.

"Now let's assume during that same year there was an inflation rate of 8 percent; that same $10,000 will lose $800 in real purchasing power during that one-year period it was tied up. Therefore, while you grossed $600 in interest income, you would net, after taxes and inflation, an actual loss of $368.

"The $368 loss is derived by taking the $600 in interest you earned and subtracting the $168 for taxes and $800 you lost due to inflation. That is a true net loss of 3.68 percent; or in other words, your original $10,000, after taxes and inflation, is now worth $9,632. That means that you are not growing at all, but in fact, going backwards. When inflation runs in double digits, this illustration becomes even more dramatic, and you must understand this well so you don't lose a lot of ground during high interest/high inflation periods.

"Even in an environment of 6 percent interest and 5 percent inflation, you still will lose money on the interest you earned, because of the taxes you will have to pay on that interest. This means that every time you take a step forward, you take two steps backwards. It's no wonder so many people find it so hard to get ahead."

Mr. Kane paused and took a deep breath, releasing it very slowly, then said, "Now, Mr. Langston, here is the real problem with inflation. Your whole economic system is taught on a number versus value basis. You are taught to think in terms of the numbers of dollars you spend, not in terms of the values of what those dollars will buy, as if the value of a dollar always stays constant.

"Have you ever taken the monthly payment on your home loan and multiplied by twelve months, then by thirty years, and thought, *My goodness! I'm paying $600,000 for a $300,000 loan!?* As you did this, were you thinking in terms of the number of dollars you spent or the value of those dollars?"

"If you are asking me personally, I am thinking I am going

to spend six hundred thousand of my hard-earned dollars. What else is there?" I replied.

Mr. Kane smiled and said, "Mr. Langston, try this new way of calculating your house loan. Assuming 8 percent inflation, the rule of 72 reveals that everything will cost twice as much in nine years, or that the value of a dollar will be one-half.

"Take your loan payment this month and multiply by 12 to get this year's cost. Use this amount for the next nine years. Then in nine years take that same amount at fifty cents on the dollar. In eighteen years it will be twenty-five cents on the dollar, and in twenty-seven years, twelve and a half cents. Now take your first nine years (pure interest, no principal period) where you used 100 percent on the dollar and take into account that because your home interest is deductible, Uncle Sam pays twenty-eight cents of every dollar for you, assuming 28 percent is your average tax rate. Therefore, it really cost you only seventy-two cents per dollar.

"With this new method of calculating the true value of your payment dollars over time, you probably won't feel so bad about the total number of dollars you paid over the thirty years of your loan. In other words, if you had a $300,000 loan that you thought was costing you $600,000 in payments, let's look at what the true value of that $600,000 is in value-adjusted dollars over the life of the loan based on these assumptions:

"Years 1 through 9: each $1 paid equals $0.72 in real value. Years 10 through 18: each $1 paid equals $0.50 in real value before considering the tax savings from the interest portion of your payment. Years 19 through 27: each $1 paid equals $0.25 in real value. And in years 28 through 30: each $1 paid equals $0.125 in real value.

"Now add up your payments using the formula I have given you and see what this loan really costs you in the value of dollars you spent. Additionally, now estimate what your home would be worth thirty years from now based on that same inflation rate. I bet you don't feel as bad as you did when you looked at this on a pure number-of-dollars basis with no regard to the real purchasing value of each dollar in the year actually spent.

"Or to look at it another way, your mortgage company gave you money on the day you made the loan to buy a house when that money was worth 100 percent of whatever those dollars would buy on that day. Then you spend the next thirty years giving them back money in payments on your loan that buy less and less every year. If they took the sum of all of your payments thirty years from now and tried to buy a house, how much smaller of a home would those severely discounted dollars buy?

"If this number-versus-value-of-the-dollar concept is still not clear to you, let me give you another example.

Suppose I handed you a $10,000 gift certificate; think how you would feel."

"I'd feel great! In fact, why don't you give it a try so I can see just how great?" I joked.

"Now," Mr. Kane said, ignoring my comment, "if we change the date I gave you this gift to the year 2045, how would you feel about receiving this same $10,000 then?"

I chuckled and said, "Obviously, I don't think you are as generous as I did a minute ago."

"However," he continued, "what if the year were changed in this example to the year 1931? My goodness! What could you buy with $10,000 in 1931, during the Great Depression, besides a new home, plus a car?

"Do you see what I mean, Mr. Langston? Money has a direct value which corresponds to the year in which you spend it. Because money has no constant value, and the rate of its value is continuously changing, many of the financial rules we were taught to operate under are no longer valid.

"One of the major financial problems for most people is trying to plan for their future. Unfortunately, because most people are still operating on a number-of-dollars basis instead of the value-of-dollars basis, they will find that at retirement that they will come up substantially short in what they need.

"In your long-term projections, please don't lock down the value of money as if it will buy the same thing in twenty or thirty years from now as it buys today. Fourteen-dollar movie tickets would have seemed impossible to someone forty-five years ago paying only $0.50.

"In fact, Mr. Langston, imagine that I could put you into a time machine and send you back to 1969 to find yourself standing in a movie line. How easy would it be for you to have a conversation with yourself and convince yourself that in forty-five years you would be paying $13—twenty-six times more—for the same ticket?

"Today, you currently have the exact same opportunity, but with 20/20 hindsight. Can you talk to yourself and try to convince yourself that the movie ticket you are paying $13 for today will probably cost you close to $340, forty-five years from now?

"You must prepare yourself for the fact that your true future retirement needs twenty to forty years out will appear just as impossible when you view them today as $13 movie tickets would have seemed to you when looking from a 1969 perspective.

"Once you start to unravel the secrets of the science of financial management, you will see that to succeed often means going against the apparent, natural flow. But fortunately, some simple changes in philosophy are capable of contributing to massive differences at the end of the game."

10

TO PLAN OR NOT
TO PLAN . . .

Lunch was over, and Mr. Kane said, "Please take a walk with me, Mr. Langston."

As we began to walk, he said, "I said a few minutes ago that the vast majority of all people in the United States will fail to provide adequately for their own secure retirement. This staggering statistic is impossible to ignore, because it's a fact that most will become dependent upon Social Security and/or our children.

"This leaves only a very small percentage who will successfully plan to provide a sufficient amount of income to support them at retirement. What incredible odds these are against your personal financial success.

"How is it possible for most to fail, when we see so much apparent wealth around us?

"One reason is all too simple. It matters little whether you make $100,000 a year or $250,000 a year if at the end of that year you have spent all of that money and have placed none of it in an area that can accrue as future income. The person making $250,000 who spends all of his or her money on cars, homes, boats, and jewelry, and has none of his or her money growing, faces the day when his or her income ceases, and cease it will. So then will his or her lifestyle.

"The first rule for establishing any form of retirement program is that you must keep a portion of what you earn for the future. You must invest a portion of each year's income. And I don't mean save it in a mattress, Mr. Langston; invest it!

"Consider two individuals who, at age fifty-one, have seemingly identical lifestyles. Each lives in a sixteen-room house in the most desirable neighborhood in the city. Each person has two children who are attending private, well-respected universities. Both families own several expensive automobiles. Both homes are furnished with only the best furniture and decorations.

"With all the apparent similarity, the difference is that one person is struggling each month to maintain his visible lifestyle. This person has a negative cash flow and incurs more debt each month to support his standard of living. He struggles to support his present way of life and gives almost no thought to any future financial plans. The other person in our example supports his visible lifestyle with a solid, positive cash flow. His current lifestyle is secured by wise investments, which also have secured his financial future.

"How did the difference between the two people occur?

Thirty years earlier, each completed his chosen training and entered work. The first person used his above-average income to buy a large house and a nice car. He committed all his income to the loan payments necessary to provide him with these possessions.

"In the next few years, his income had increased to a point that permitted him to finance a boat and a more expensive car. Again, he committed his entire income, after taxes, to loan payments, which provided for his material surroundings. This man continued each year to enjoy very healthy increases in his income, but he used the increased flow of cash to support higher and higher loans and mortgage payments. He continued this pattern until his interest and tax payments today have overtaken his inflow of cash.

"The other person developed a different pattern of living, beginning with his first year of work. Instead of using all his newly generated first-year income on the purchase of material goods, he began a disciplined investment program. He set aside a fixed amount of income each month to invest in some safe, but growing, investment area. Each time that he was fortunate enough to realize an increase in his income, he increased the amount of his regularly scheduled investment dollars. After several years, his first investments had increased in value and provided enough earnings for him to purchase a larger home and nicer furniture. Each year thereafter his investments generated additional income for him to use toward acquiring those items that provided him with an improved style of living. However, he always reinvested a portion of his investment earnings along with his additionally increased income. In essence, he was buying his luxuries with investment returns and not destroying current income.

"As he invested and reinvested, his cash flow position became very secure. He could buy practically whatever he wanted from investment earnings and still know that his financial future was secure.

"Our friend's investment pattern resembles the creation of a family. The original investments, the parents, ultimately generate earnings, the children. The earnings, or children, are reinvested, and they too generate more earnings after a period of time. As the earnings, children and grandchildren, multiply, the individual generates more and more opportunity for earnings, or more children. The effect is a widespread base for current and future financial security. If he uses only the children or grandchildren for his lifestyle, he still grows stronger each day. Today when this person looks back over his thirty-year productive history, he sees he still has some of the original capital working for him each year from thirty years ago to the present. Meanwhile, the first person has consumed each year's income and has nothing left but tomorrow's labor.

"All that meets the eye does not necessarily make the entire picture. In this story you have significant insight into the differences between financial success and failure.

"Lack of adequate planning is another reason for failure, Mr. Langston. Consider the twenty-four-year-old who, back in 1950, decided to set up her retirement plan. In a visit with the executives of her corporation, she found that her employer was contributing $40 a month toward her retirement through corporate profit sharing and a pension plan. The executives also projected that this contribution would be worth $100 a month in retirement benefits at age sixty-five.

"Next she met with her life insurance agent, who sold

her an insurance policy for which she paid $50-a-month premiums. At age sixty-five, she would be able to withdraw (from cash values) $65 a month for the rest of her life. She also checked with Social Security and learned that it was paying present recipients $43 a month.

"Now her retirement plan was set. She would receive at her retirement $215 a month, which back in 1950 represented a reasonable income for a person of sixty-five. Remember, my friend: the median family income in 1950 was about $3,000 a year, or $250 per month.

"She then puts her nose to the grindstone and she doesn't look up again until she's sixty-five. The year in this example would be 1991, and she receives, as promised from the corporate profit sharing and pension plan, $100 a month. Her insurance policy also pays out $65 a month, but Social Security has increased from $43 to about $800 a month in that year.

"Now she is receiving approximately $1,000 a month. But it is 1991 and very difficult to live on $1,000 a month. Even more tragically, her $1,000 a month will not increase as much as inflation does. Each successive year her lifestyle will therefore be reduced. Eventually she will find it nearly impossible to survive.

"Here was a person who did some planning, but failed to foresee the changing elements that could affect her long-term financial goals.

"Why do 95 percent of all people fail to reach their financial goals and only 5 percent succeed? What is it the 5 percent know about accomplishing goals that the other 95 percent do not know? Let me assume, Mr. Langston, you wish to retire at age sixty-five with a comfortable income, say, $6,000 a month at today's standard of living; to develop an education plan that will provide sufficient funds for your children's education; and to have financial security from any impending disasters that could beset you or your family, such as death, disability, or serious illness.

"Further imagine that you have just received the telegram we discussed earlier telling you that a rich uncle of yours has died in Hawaii and all of your financial goals have been left to you, with no strings attached. The only requirement is that you must go and pick them up in Hawaii.

"Let's look at how various people may approach obtaining this goal. I am sure you would find some that are so impulsive and nearsighted that they might go to the edge of San Francisco Bay, jump in, and start swimming toward Hawaii. Obviously these people are doomed before they even start.

"However, the vast majority are smart enough to buy some type of boat." Mr. Kane took another napkin and drew the following illustration as he continued. "And some of them might even buy navigational equipment. After setting the compass heading south-southwest for Hawaii, they would set sail, never considering that five miles from shore, they would no longer have any visual bearings. A compass heading of south-southwest would be absolutely useless once in the ocean's currents and winds got hold of their boat and started pushing it around the ocean. The chances of reaching Hawaii even in this scenario would also be nil because if you miss Hawaii by a few miles on the water, you will sail right by it and never see it. As you continue to sail, you will ultimately end up in Japan, which is farther away from Hawaii than you were back in San Francisco.

"These absurd illustrations should remind you of a method undertaken by 95 percent in the attempted achievement of their

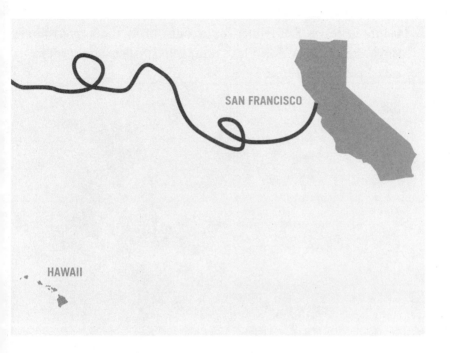

financial goals. They are either blindly reaching for dreams or inadequately planning their journey.

"However, professional ship captains set sail for Hawaii every day and arrive 99.9 percent of the time. Therefore, it might bear asking what the ship's captain is doing differently than these others in our illustration.

"The answer is a ship's captain acts according to his experience and training," Mr. Kane said as he took yet another napkin and drew the following diagram. "He charts a course from San Francisco to Hawaii that is a series of coordinate points from San Francisco to Hawaii. He does this because he realizes his navigational equipment cannot sail from San Francisco all the way across the ocean to Hawaii in a single step. Therefore, before he leaves San Francisco, he must break the impossible single-step journey down into numerous smaller sub-journeys, called *coordinate points.*

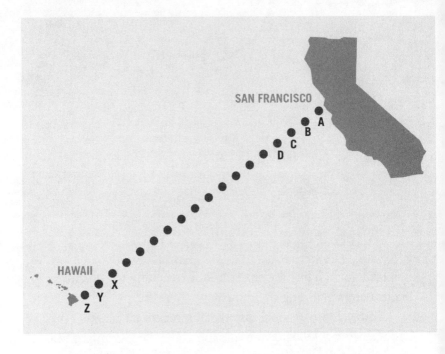

"Then when he leaves the port of San Francisco, his only focus is on getting to coordinate point A, which is the first coordinate point on his course. When he arrives at coordinate point A and verifies that he is there, he then proceeds to coordinate point B, and so on, through C, D, E, F, his last coordinate point being the port in Hawaii. Then, and only then, has he accomplished what he set out to do.

"If along his journey he is blown off course, he can return to the nearest coordinate point and proceed along the charted course.

Or, he can identify his present position and plot a new course.

"It is the lack of this step-by-step procedure that causes failures in the financial plans of most people.

"You may think that you have your personal retirement plan completely set up and expect to be among the 5 percent of the people who succeed at providing for a secure retirement. If so, Mr. Langston, answer these questions for yourself:

"At what age do you plan to retire?

"How much income, at today's standard of living, will you require to live comfortably in retirement?

"Considering inflation, how much income will you need in the year you plan to retire in order to provide the lifestyle you have specified as of today?

"How large an estate will you need, in dollars and cents, to produce, at a nominal rate of return, the monthly income that you will need then?

"How much do you have to invest each year between now and then to build that estate so it will provide sufficient retirement income for you at your projected retirement date?

"Finally, have you used a reasonable rate of inflation in your entire projected retirement program?

"If you do not have satisfactory answers to all these questions, Mr. Langston, then you do not have an adequate retirement plan. Until you can answer each of these questions, you have not even identified Hawaii as the target of your journey. Not knowing where you are trying to go, once you set sail from San Francisco, makes the completion of any such journey impossible.

"Remember that financial management is a science interwoven with other sciences. This method of goal planning is nothing more than an application of the science of navigation.

The science of navigation not only applies to accomplishing financial goals, but applies to accomplishing anything you ever set out to do.

"A surgeon uses the science of navigation to complete every operation successfully. He starts with a well-planned first incision and follows a step-by-step procedure that concludes with the last suture.

"The same is true of an attorney who plans out how he wants to present his case to the jury, all the way down to his final summation. Doesn't a CPA start with an initial form to create a tax return and then follow a series of predetermined steps until the last form is completed so all information can then be transferred to the front page of the return?

"All professionals employ this science of navigation to develop a successful conclusion to any complicated procedure. Therefore, you too must establish the idea that you will accomplish your goals by a designated plan and not by accident. You should develop the plan with enough flexibility so that you can adjust to changes (personal, financial, emotional, and physical) in your internal environment. You must also be able to adjust to changes in the external environment (changes in our tax laws, fluctuating inflation rates, and a volatile national and international economy). In short, the correct plan today may not be the correct plan tomorrow. Remember, Mr. Langston: proper financial management requires continuing evaluation, because no part of anyone's economic situation stays constant."

11

SPENDING TIME

By now we were back at the front of the inn, and Mr. Kane said, "Mr. Langston, please get in the cab. I want to take you somewhere." I got into the cab and he started driving toward the west end of the island.

"No study of personal wealth-building strategies is complete without a discussion of the management of time," he said. "Too often we are concerned with the number of hours available for productive output rather than maximizing the output during those available hours. We tend to believe that the physical units of time limit the amount of productive output that we can accomplish. This is not always true. In fact, statistical data usually point to the opposite.

"To make the most of our available time, we need to know what achievements will have the greatest impact on our present goals. Most successful managers have a way of accomplishing this. To solve persistent problems, business and technical managers must collect large bodies of data. One tool frequently used in analyzing large quantities of data is the *80/20 rule*, sometimes referred to as the *Pareto principle*. J. M. Juran, a well-known quality consultant, named the Pareto principle after an Italian economist who formulated some relationships about the distribution of wealth in his country. His study showed that the majority of wealth was controlled by only a few families. Juran also called this the *principle of the vital few and the trivial many*.

"To solve persistent problems, managers want to concentrate their resources on those solutions that offer the greatest cost reductions and, consequently, the greatest profit increases. In almost all cases the problems that generate the majority of the costs are limited to a 'vital few.' By concentrating his problem-solving efforts on those few problem areas, the manager can maximize his time and problem-solving costs.

"All of us probably can benefit from an application of the 80/20 rule to our own daily time scheduling. Ask yourself, Mr. Langston, 'How do I decide how much time to spend on a particular task? Is it dictated to me by an established routine? Do I respond to the next person in line or to the person who speaks the loudest to get my attention?' In most situations, a little advance planning will help you achieve vastly improved results.

"If two tasks are at hand, both requiring the same amount of time to accomplish, which is accomplished first? If the priorities are well defined, then the decision is easy. Many times, however, it will be beneficial to list all the tasks, clients, and appointments, anything requiring time. Then rank the list according to the time required to accomplish the task, versus the results achieved. Results can be quantified in terms of income generated or costs reduced. The results of the initial analysis usually demonstrate that one spends a majority of his time generating relatively little income.

"These same results usually show that 80 percent of a person's income (if he works on a fee basis) is generated in 20 percent of his working time. With a clear set of objectives, and good planning, an individual can fill the majority of his available time with only those tasks that have the greatest impact on increasing income or reducing costs. This is the ratio of 20 percent time to 80 percent income. If you analyze your day, Mr. Langston, I believe you may be shocked at how accurate this formula truly is. The key to time management is discipline and delegation.

"First, recognize that there are only twenty-four hours in a day and only seven days in a week. Nothing you do can change how many hours a week in which you have to work. In my method of time management, I prefer to work only by the day within the week rather than the week as a whole. Since I have only twenty-four hours in a day, there are some basic necessities, such as eating and sleeping, that have to be taken care of during those twenty-four hours. The rest of the time is mine, and I am dedicated to making the most use of the time I have. I want to work some, enjoy my family some, and have some time left for myself.

"If I have chosen to spend eight hours each day working, that period becomes a fixed denominator. If 20 percent of my time makes 80 percent of my money, and vice versa, what would happen if I successfully identified the 20 percent of my activities that makes the 80 percent of my income? If I then spent 40 percent of my time working in those areas, would I make twice as much money? You bet!

"Let me show you a simple illustration using some of the allergists with whom I have worked when I was in practice. Most had incomes between $275,000 and $300,000 a year. But I can remember one who made $800,000 a year and another who made only $100,000 a year. Using these last two as an example, they both spent the same amount of time a day working and had comparable fees. Therefore, how can one allergist make $800,000 a year while the other makes only $100,000?

"The doctor who made $100,000 believed in 'the personal touch'; he performed each set of allergy tests himself, and then visited with each patient as the patient dressed and waited on the results. In addition, he personally gave all of his patients their injections. The other fellow did nothing during the day that didn't require his MD capabilities. He had eight patients at a time receive their tests from eight registered nurses in eight different examining rooms. Because allergy tests can be competently performed by nurses but require an MD to read the results, he simply popped in when needed to read those results and prescribe the appropriate treatment. The nurses, fully qualified, then gave the injections.

"As another example, an ophthalmologist makes 20 percent of her money for the 80 percent of her time doing eye exams in the office, while she makes 80 percent of her money for the 20 percent of her time doing eye surgery. 'But,' you say, 'she has to perform those eye exams to get the surgeries, right?' Wrong! If she delegated eye exams to an optician on her payroll at $50 an hour, she would increase her payroll cost, but free up more time to spend in the operating room at $500 to $1,000 an hour. In other words, doing eye exams makes her work at the level of productivity and profit of an optician, $50 per hour, rather than as the highly trained eye surgeon, where she is making $500 to $1,000 per hour.

"If she then chooses to reconcile her own checkbook, she becomes a bookkeeper worth $20 an hour; if she runs her daily receipts to the bank for deposit, she becomes an $8-an-hour messenger person. In short, if she has only eight hours a day to work and delegates everything to a subordinate, who doesn't require her MD expertise to perform, think of how much more income she can generate in the same eight hours.

"While these two examples both used physicians, this works the same in any field. Everyone has their own 80/20 rule that applies to what they do. If you want to get ahead, you need to maximize what you can produce with the hours you choose to devote to work.

"Time is a precious commodity, Mr. Langston, not to be abused or wasted. Its management is essential for your success. You cannot overexaggerate the value of practicing this philosophy in your life."

12

GEOMETRIC PROGRESSION VERSUS ADDITION

"Now it's time for a little review," Mr. Kane said, "because what I tell you next depends on your having grasped what we have already discussed.

"Remember how I said that financial management is a science?"

"Yes," I replied.

"Well, like any science, it must be studied to be understood. Nothing happens by accident. Success is a result of proper planning and implementation of sound financial concepts. In fact, what looks right on the surface, may be the opposite once thoroughly evaluated.

"Mr. Langston, what did J. Paul Getty, Aristotle Onassis, Howard Hughes, and Trammell Crow all have in common? They all carefully exploited a concept called *OPM*, or what is commonly referred to as leverage."

"What does OPM stand for?" I asked.

"Other People's Money," Mr. Kane answered. "Each of these men understood that he could never create a financial dynasty using only what he could earn through hourly wages. Instead, each of these men used leverage to build his empire."

"Wait a minute," I interjected. "I have always been taught that borrowing money was wrong. In fact, my father always said, 'If you don't have the money in your pocket, don't buy it.' Isn't leverage just another fancy word for borrowing money?"

"A lot of people seem to think so," Mr. Kane answered, "and so did I until I started to study the habits of wealthy people like the ones I just named. In fact, in the process of doing so, I also discovered another popular use of leverage, and like OPM, it was also responsible for numerous fortunes being made in the last several decades. It's called *network marketing*. In network marketing, instead of exchanging an hour of your labor for an hour's pay, you leverage your efforts by helping others improve their financial destiny. This way, instead of your earnings being limited based on how many hours you can work, you receive compensation based on all the people that you help, plus help them help, and so on. I will tell you more about this in a few minutes.

"You can see how either concept may be contrary to what you have been taught based on popular clichés such as: 'Always pay cash; never borrow' or 'Better to get a salaried job so you'll have some security.'

"You see, Mr. Langston, once I started studying how others

had made their fortunes, I started to see that there are many areas where commonly accepted philosophies are not always the best. Let me try to help you make more sense of the issue of leverage by focusing on the purchase of a home as an example.

"There are really only two ways in which you may purchase a home. You may pay cash for it, or you may mortgage it. If you decide to mortgage it, there are a variety of options. You may pay anywhere from 5 percent to 95 percent of the value in cash at closing, and you may finance the balance anywhere from one year to thirty years. Which is better? A one-year mortgage with 95 percent down, or a thirty-year mortgage with 5 percent down?"

I started to answer, when Mr. Kane interrupted me, saying, "Before you can answer this, you need a scale by which to measure all your financial transactions. Therefore, let's use the scale of one to ten, where one will be the worst that you could achieve with your money, and ten will be the best.

"To start, let's assume that you have $250,000 in the bank and want to buy a $250,000 home. This gives you the option of an outright purchase for cash. Mr. Langston, whenever you make a major financial decision, borrow a secret from Ben Franklin. Old Ben said that anytime you had to make an important decision, the easiest way to decide was to draw a big *T* on a piece of paper." With that Mr. Kane pulled the cab to the side of the road. He then drew a big *T* on a white notepad that was attached by a suction cup to the windshield of the cab. Then he began to write as he spoke. "Over the horizontal bar of the *T*, write an *A* on the left-hand side and write a *D* over the right-hand side of the bar; the *A* stands for advantages, the *D* for disadvantages." His drawing looked like this:

Benjamin Franklin's T

A	D
1. Title in own possession	1. Investment eroded by inflation
2. No interest	2. Funds not available for investment
3. No monthly payment	3. Potential difficulty in selling
4. Repossession out of the question	4. No tax benefits

"Next," he went on, "consider all of the reasons why you should do what you are contemplating; then think of all the reasons not to do what you are contemplating. Rarely is a decision completely clear-cut. The only way to determine which decision to make is to weigh the advantages against the disadvantages. The winner will select itself.

"Mr. Langston, what are benefits of paying the total purchase price in cash?"

I thought, and then gave him the major reasons I could come up with to pay cash for a home. "Number one, you would have the title free and clear; number two, no interest on a loan; number three, no monthly house payments; number four, the house cannot be repossessed."

Mr. Kane said, "Those are all excellent advantages for paying cash for your home, can you think of any more?"

I paused a moment to think and then said, "No, those are the main ones."

"OK," Mr. Kane said. "Now, weigh those against the disadvantages. You have taken $250,000, lifted the house up, and you placed the $250,000 beneath the foundation and left it there to be eroded by inflation for as long as you live in that house.

If the long-term inflation rate was 6 percent, and you lived in the house for twelve years before selling it, the $250,000 you would get back from the sale would be worth only $125,000 in today's purchasing power."

"Wait a minute," I interrupted. "That's not totally true. The house is appreciating due to inflation."

"Some people argue that point, and in most situations, if they bought a home in a growing neighborhood, the house will appreciate. But that house will appreciate with or without a mortgage. The fact that you paid $250,000 cash for the house will not increase the value of your house in the marketplace.

"By paying cash, you are taking $250,000 from your investment portfolio. Assume that instead of using this capital for the house, you invested the $250,000 in something that paid a 6 percent tax-free return, or an 8.3 percent taxable return. This means that your $250,000 within the same twelve-year period would have grown to $500,000.

"After twelve years you could sell your investment, retire the $250,000 mortgage, and still have $250,000 or more for continued investment. If you paid cash for the house, the only thing you could ever have is the house. By investing the money, you have an option of growth plus the house. That growth may be used someday to completely pay off your home and realize a surplus.

"If the inflation rate is higher than the net cost of borrowing, the interest you paid less any tax savings received, Mr. Langston, will achieve an additional economic benefit by delaying the principal payment on that loan.

"The dollar that you have in your pocket today is probably the most valuable dollar that you will have for the rest of your life. Do you want to pay that dollar today in the form of principal on a home payment, or would you rather wait thirty years, when the value of that dollar may be worth only one-tenth of its value today, and pay it against the principal of the same home mortgage?"

I didn't have to think at all to answer that; I said, "Give me the thirty years."

"You see, Mr. Langston," he continued, "paying cash for your home obviously would rate very low on a scale of one to ten—say, around two."

"How do you get a one?" I asked.

Mr. Kane chuckled and answered, "Fully mortgage the home; then take the $250,000 to Las Vegas and lose it on the gambling tables, or just blow it on your lifestyle. Then you would have a $250,000 mortgage and nothing left for investment. Don't make the mistake, Mr. Langston, of thinking I'm saying mortgage everything for the sake of borrowing. *This concept only works if you prudently invest the money.*"

I thought about that and said, "This is beginning to make sense to me. If I invested my money instead of putting it into my house, then my investment's growth can later pay off the mortgage. Then I not only would have the original investment, but also a free-and-clear home." Then I said, "How do you climb up the scale, Mr. Kane?"

Mr. Kane answered my question with another question. "Is a 5 percent down payment better than a 30 percent down payment? If paying today's valuable cash for a home is the wrong thing to do, then it also would be wrong to make any larger down payment than is absolutely required by the mortgage company. Shop around, Mr. Langston. Talk with various mortgage companies and compare rates. Select the one that offers the lowest down payment and longest period of loan. Don't worry about the one-half percent or 1 percent difference in interest rates; it's one of the last tax deductions left. The lower down payment and longer loan period will make up the one-half percent or 1 percent in the long run. With inflation acting as your friend, you will repay the loan with cheaper dollars.

"Now, when it comes time to decide the exact length of the loan; the longer the term, the better. Let me give you an example. Take a person who built a home in 1956 and spent $15,000 in construction costs. He then fully mortgaged the home, with a house payment of about $150 a month. Assume that this person's monthly income was $600 in 1956, which was a respectable income in that year. This means that the house payment represented his single largest expense, 25 percent. The groceries probably cost no more than $40 a month, the telephone cost $5 a month, and gasoline was 18 cents a gallon.

"Twenty-five years later, if this person wished, he could probably sell his home for $150,000. The house he built in 1956 for just $15,000 was on a three-quarter-acre lot and had four bedrooms. In 1981, it cost $150,000 in most cities to duplicate it. But what happened to his house payment? It was still $150 a month. His gasoline bill on the car ran $125 a month. His telephone bill was $60, the monthly utilities on the house were $400, and his grocery bill was more than $500 a month.

"While the house payment stayed constant, the value of the payment had declined to the point that it no longer makes up a significant percentage of his monthly expenses. From this example it becomes clear that the longer you delay the payment on the fixed mortgage, the better the outcome."

I thought about this concept for a few minutes and then said, "It appears, from what you are saying, the banks are really losing money on longterm financing due to inflation. Is this why so many banks failed during the 1980s and again in 2009?"

Mr. Kane laughed out loud and said, "No, my dear friend, absolutely not. Their problems were based on other factors. In fact, where do you think the banks get their money?"

I thought and said, "The government? . . . No, from the deposits of the savers."

"Very good, Mr. Langston!" Mr. Kane complimented. "The bankers are not really the lenders, but instead are borrowers themselves. They borrow money from the saving depositors at a low rate and then loan it out at a higher rate. The bank makes its profits on the spread between the two rates. Inflation doesn't hurt the bank, Mr. Langston; inflation hurts the saver who is being paid interest on his money at a rate less than inflation. People must learn to manage their money properly, earning yields higher than inflation, if they want to get ahead."

"So, you are telling me I probably want to be in debt . . . right?" I asked, a bit unsure of myself.

"Absolutely not, Mr. Langston!" Mr. Kane answered. "I am in no way suggesting that you go out and charge up a bunch of things you can't afford on your credit cards. That is the fastest way I know to financial disaster. In fact, borrowing money to buy personal assets is usually not a good philosophy at all."

"OK, now I'm good and confused," I said.

"So was I when I was first trying to figure this all out for myself," Mr. Kane replied. "I went back and forth on this 'whether or not to borrow' issue and remained quite confused until I finally created a little formula to help me sort it all out. It was during the process of developing this formula that I actually realized that there are two types of debt. The first I will call 'good debt' and the second 'bad debt.' Some debt should be paid off as soon as possible, while other debt should be extended as long as possible. Mr. Langston, let me share my little formula with you so that you determine when your debt is good debt or bad debt.

"You see, good debt is when the debt actually makes you a profit; bad debt is when it costs you money."

"How can debt ever make you a profit?" I asked.

Mr. Kane answered, "That is best revealed by understanding my good debt/bad debt formula." He then wrote it down for me:

Debt is justified anytime the <u>net cost of the debt</u> (the interest you pay) is less than the <u>net income earned through investments</u> made with the money borrowed, <u>plus any benefits of inflation</u>.

"Now, let's go back to our home mortgage discussion to see how this formula works." Mr. Kane removed the top sheet from his note holder and began drawing the following chart, filling it in as he explained.

HOME MORTGAGE DEBT
"Good Debt" v. "Bad Debt" Formula

Interest Costs (5%)	−5%
Tax Savings (28%)	1.4%
Investment Income	4.6%
Inflation	3.5%
Net Gain/Loss	4.5%
Net Gain	4.5%

"Say you can get a thirty-year fixed-rate loan for 5 percent. Another example of this same issue is whether to take a thirty-year loan, or make higher payments so you can get your loan paid off in ten to fifteen years. Both examples are really asking the same question: doesn't it make sense to put your excess money into your home mortgage to reduce your total interest costs on your loan? My good debt\bad debt formula provides the answer.

"The way you use the formula is to first take the interest of 5 percent, which is our costs. Because it's a home loan, your interest is tax deductible. This means if the last dollars you earned were taxed at the 28 percent tax bracket, then Uncle Sam will refund 28 percent of the 5 percent in interest you paid, or the equivalent 1.41 percent. Therefore, your net cost of this interest is really only 3.6 percent.

"Now, let's say you invested the extra money you didn't use on the down payment, or in higher house payments, into a very conservative investment, like a AAA-rated municipal bond, which, say, earned 4.6 percent tax-free. Your 4.6 percent bond interest will pay all of the net loan costs of 3.6 percent, leaving you a 1 percent profit, but that's before adding the extra profit generated by inflation.

"Remember back in my savings example, when I showed you how inflation was our enemy? It took away from our investment's earning power. But when you borrow money, the dollar the banker gives you today will buy more than the dollar you pay him back later. This is due to the very same principle.

"So to wrap things up, we take the profit we earn from inflation, which let's say is 3.5 percent this year, and add it to the 1 percent profit we got by subtracting our net interest cost from our net investment earnings, and we have a 4.5 percent gain. Mr. Langston, that's a 4.5 percent profit, after tax and after inflation.

"Now, my friend, would you like to guess what your bank would have had to pay you in interest on a savings account for you to have netted 4.5 percent after taxes and inflation?"

I had no earthly idea.

"The answer is, 11.1 percent interest," he said, smiling.

"*What?*" I almost shouted.

"That's right," he continued. "If you had earned 11.1 percent in the 28 percent tax bracket, you would have to pay 3.1 percent in taxes, leaving you 8 percent. If you then deducted a 3.5 percent loss in purchasing power for inflation, you would have about 4.5 percent left after taxes and inflation.

"And what is more important, let's not forget that in this example, we are assuming some of the lowest interest, inflation, and safe investment rates in decades. Additionally, the home loan interest, which is our only cost or disadvantage in this scenario, is locked down for the next thirty years. But inflation and investment yield, for our two friends in this example, are most probably going to go up substantially during the next thirty-year period. These future increases will mean significant additional profits. So, my friend, this is a great example of what I mean by 'good debt.'

"Now," he continued, as he tore off that page and started a new chart, "let me give you an example of bad debt. Suppose you borrowed money you did not have to buy some clothes on your credit card and the interest was 18.5 percent.

"Credit card interest is no longer tax deductible, so the interest costs you the full 18.5 percent. Since you bought clothes with money you didn't have, there isn't any money left over to

HOME MORTGAGE DEBT
"Good Debt" v. "Bad Debt" Formula

Interest Costs (18.5%)	−18.5%
Tax Savings (28%)	0%
Investment Income	0%
Inflation	3.5%
Net Gain/Loss	−15%
Net Loss	−15%

invest, so your net investment income is zero. However, inflation is still your friend in this example, so at the assumed rate of inflation of 3.5 percent, the net cost of borrowing is still a −15 percent. That is a very real loss of 15 percent, which is what I call *very* bad debt."

This whole concept was beginning to distort everything I had ever been taught about money. I didn't feel comfortable with the thought that borrowing money, for any reason, may be right, but I couldn't dispute Mr. Kane's logic. Then it dawned on me which one of us was the billionaire and which wasn't.

Mr. Kane, sensing my inner turmoil, said, "Mr. Langston, this is probably one of the most difficult concepts to swallow because it goes against everything most of us are taught. But the philosophies you were taught only look at a portion of the picture. I have just changed your vantage point, in effect shifted your paradigm, if you will. And now you are looking at more of the total picture. You are including more of the real factors that affect this transaction, such as inflation, time, and income taxes."

He paused, and then said, "Mr. Langston, do you remember earlier today when we were at the pond and I asked you to look ahead and tell me everything you saw, and then I asked you to turn around and do it again? That same example also works to explain what we have just done here through a paradigm shift.

"You see, sometimes a very simple shift in vantage point opens up a much bigger picture than you originally could see. At the pond you hadn't moved at all. But instead of only looking forward, like a horse with blinders on, you were also able to turn around, and you gained a much broader perspective of all that surrounded you."

"I really do think I understand what you saying now," I said. "However, to make sure, what if I can afford to pay cash for my house and I want the freedom of knowing I don't have any debt to worry about. Should I still finance?"

Mr. Kane took a deep breath and said, "That is a very good question. If you have the money to pay cash for your home, there is a certain peace of mind in knowing nothing can ever happen that could cause you to lose it. If you also have all of the money you will ever need for your retirement and don't need to grow any more financially, I would say that you should do whatever makes you feel most comfortable. After all, what good is having money if you can't enjoy its benefits?"

Mr. Kane started the cab and drove down to the beach to a little thatched-roof structure. It was a small island café, called Nioa's Place, and it looked like a large lean-to. The western side of the structure was completely open and presented a beautiful view of the ocean to its patrons. Mr. Kane and I went inside and ordered coffee. When the waiter left, Mr. Kane continued his discourse.

"This next concept, Mr. Langston, is one of the most powerful in personal financial management; it relates to the effect that geometric progression has on your money.

"Using the rule of 72 that I taught you earlier, and knowing our projected rate of growth, we can determine how long it will take for our money to double in value, or in the case of inflation, to become worth one-half. Now, let me show you the effects of this progression as your money doubles and doubles again." He took a napkin and drew the following illustration:

1, 2, 4, 8, 16, 32, 64, 128, 256, 512

"Mr. Langston, there are two important points to see about this progression. First, any form of positive growth, no matter how small, will produce this exact progression. The only question becomes, how many years will it take for each number to double? One growing into two is the same growth as 256 growing into 512, with both initial numbers simply doubled. But where would you like to be in this progression? Do you want to start today with your first dollar being invested to grow into the two dollars? Or, if you started a long time ago, today you could be investing $256,000 to watch it double to $512,000."

"I'd rather be at the $256,000 point!"

"Good." he said. "Now another important point to recognize is that time is the biggest factor in growth. If your investments are growing at a 12 percent annual rate, you can use the rule of 72 and can find that every six years your entire investment asset base will double."

Mr. Kane then drew the following diagram on the napkin and continued.

"As you can see, if you start with $20,000 at age thirty-six, you will have doubled it to $40,000 by age forty-two. By age forty-eight it will be $80,000, at age fifty-four it will be $160,000, and finally, by sixty, around the time of retirement, it will be $320,000.

Age	Investment
36	$20,000
42	$40,000
48	$80,000
54	$160,000
60	$320,000

He then flipped the napkin over and drew this diagram, continuing to speak as he drew.

Age	Investment
30	$20,000
36	$40,000
42	$80,000
48	$160,000
54	$320,000
60	$640,000

"However, Mr. Langston, let me make here a very important and startling point. If you started this illustration just six years earlier, at age of thirty instead of thirty-six, you would have twice as much to retire with, because you would have added one full additional progression period to the beginning, which allows your money to double once more at the end. In the second example you would end up with $640,000 in a retirement corpus instead of $320,000. That's quite a difference for getting started just a little earlier. This proves that it is not how much you start with but when you start. A person who starts investing at age twenty-five from his earnings of, say, $30,000 a year can have more to retire with than someone who starts at age fifty with earnings of $150,000 a year.

"It reminds me of a question Moses once asked me. He said 'Akamai, would you rather have $1,000,000 in cash or a penny that will double in value for every square on a chess board?' Check this out for yourself, Mr. Langston, to see which you would prefer. The penny grows to a number bigger than you know how to pronounce, it is a number of dollars with twenty-seven zeros after it!

"It is not having more money to start with that is important; *it is having more time!*

"Now, do not interpret this concept as good only for thirty-year-old people. If someone is forty-five or fifty-five, is it too late? Of course not! As I just showed you, it is better to start today instead of tomorrow! If in favor of a better lifestyle you wait to start your asset accumulation for just a few years, you will pay dearly in the end, my friend."

Just then, the waiter brought our coffee. Mr. Kane took a deep sip and then said, "Another very important fact revealed in the study of financial geometric progression is the effect that your actual investment yield has on your money. Rate of return affects the time necessary for your money to double, right?"

I nodded.

"Therefore, by increasing the rate of return, you add more progressions to the same amount of time remaining.

"As you explore the effects of inflation and geometric progression, several strongly rooted financial golden rules start to crumble: 'Always pay cash.' 'Never borrow.' 'Save money for a rainy day,' with emphasis on bank savings accounts.

"These economic rules have passed from generation to generation. Today, the correct rules are just the reverse. *Learning to plan properly for your future is essential to your long-range success,* Mr. Langston."

13

BEGIN THE JOURNEY

I looked down at the sandy beach floor of the café and saw a tiny sand crab poke its head out of a hole next to my chair. I moved to get a closer look and it disappeared back into the hole. Mr. Kane had been quiet for a few minutes and was watching the surf pound the beach. And then, as if a thought had just popped into his mind, he said. "Earlier, we discussed the science of navigation. Now let's apply that science to see how to reach your specific goal of retirement.

"The first step in the science of navigation is to identify your current location. In financial management this usually means identifying your current net investment asset base. For the purpose of illustration, let's assume that your current net investment asset base at age thirty-five is $10,000.

"The second step in charting a course is to determine your destination or desired future location. This means identifying the goal itself. If retirement were the goal, this future location step would require that you determine your goal by asking the following questions.

"'At what age do I want to retire?'

"'What current monthly income would I desire if I were retiring today?'

"'What is the future monthly income, after adjusting for inflation, that I would need when my retirement actually occurs?'

"And finally, 'How large an estate would I need to have to produce the retirement income I want?'

"The amount of this newly calculated future estate therefore becomes your desired future location. In our previous navigational illustration, it was Hawaii. For this example, let's assume the future asset base we need is going to be $750,000.

"Mr. Langston, how can you turn $10,000 into $750,000 in one step legally?"

I thought for a moment, and not coming up with any way, I responded, "You can't. It's impossible. Not unless you buy ten thousand lottery tickets and happen to win."

"That is why we have to do what the captain does and break this impossible journey down into small, obtainable sub-journeys," Mr. Kane explained.

"For the sub-journeys you must ask yourself the following questions:

"How many years do I have to build my present net worth to the new desired net worth?

"What rate of return do I expect to achieve on my new investments?

"How much do I have to invest each year at the prescribed investment yield to build this new, desired estate?

"After you have resolved these three questions, Mr. Langston, the only thing left to successfully accomplish this retirement goal is to invest the predetermined amount of money for the prescribed number of years and achieve the projected rate of annual growth.

"Trying to build $750,000 in one single step appears to be an impossibility. However, with these navigational steps you find if you have thirty years until retirement and if your investments can grow at, say, 10 percent per year, the achievement of your goal will require an investment of just over $4,500 per year. That's less than $400 a month. This $4,500 investment each year for thirty years at 10 percent will build the extra $740,000 you need to make your $10,000 into $750,000.

"Mr. Langston, each of your other personal financial goals, including planning for your children's education and taking care of your family in the event of your premature death, can be accomplished using this same procedure. Do you have children?"

"Yes," I said proudly. "I have a little seven-year-old son named Trey and a brand-new daughter named Tiffany."

"That's wonderful, Mr. Langston," Mr. Kane said. "Let me show you how to design their college education plan. First you must determine the dates your children will enter college, as well as the amount of financial assistance you want to give them. You should figure the approximate cost of their education on today's basis and then apply an inflation estimate to determine the probable cost when the children enter college.

"You can do this using the rule of 72. Let's say you assume there is going to be an average of 8 percent inflation for the next twenty-five years; you simply divide eight into 72. The answer tells you that the cost of everything will double each nine years. Therefore, when your new daughter enters college in eighteen years, it will cost four times as much.

"Let's just focus on your daughter for a moment to make this as simple as possible to understand. Suppose you want to send your newborn daughter through six years of college, which today costs around $12,000 per year. Those six years at $12,000 per year equals $72,000. Unfortunately, that is the cost if your child were to attend and pay for all six years of college *today*! Since she won't enter college for eighteen years, you must compute the projected, inflated cost for college then. At our assumed 8 percent inflation—which, by the way, is conservative because the costs of college educations are escalating at a rate much higher than the average rate of inflation—the cost for the first year of college will be $48,000 instead of the $12,000 it costs today. The second year it goes to almost $52,000, then approximately $56,000 the third year. By the sixth and final year, it will cost a little over $70,000.

"This means instead of a total cost of $72,000 today, it will cost around $350,000 then, and that's the good news."

"*Good* news?!" I shouted. "How can that be *good* news? What could be worse than that?"

"Let me tell you the bad news, my friend," Mr. Kane answered. "There is nothing tax deductible about educating your children. Therefore, you will have to earn money and pay taxes on it to net the amount you need. At your average 28 percent tax bracket, you will have to earn near $490,000 in salary just to net (after paying around $140,000 in income tax) the $350,000 this child will need to pay for this college education. That means $490,000 taken out of your income stream to cover this one child's needs."

"That's incredible!" I said. "Nobody I know is thinking like this. What can I do, Mr. Kane? I can't afford that kind of money. What's the use in even trying?"

Mr. Kane responded, "Please relax, Mr. Langston. It's not as bad as it seems. You see, you just looked at all that money on the same value system as the dollar is worth today. Those are future dollars we are talking about. You remember that last year's cost of $70,000 won't be worth any more then than $12,000 is worth today. In other words, you'll be earning a lot more then. But don't let that make you lazy, Mr. Langston; we still need to plan to have $350,000, because that is what it will cost then. Let me show you what I recommend you consider doing to cover the cost of paying for your children's educations.

"Mr. Langston, you should set up a monthly investment fund and allow it to grow so it can pay for these expenses later. This way, your money can begin to work for you today and pay for tomorrow's high cost of providing your children with an education. If you do this, you will not have to work as hard to pay for every dollar.

"If you started today, because of the power of the geometric progression working on your investment dollars, a $7,200-a-year investment, made each year for the next eighteen years, would build a fund that would totally pay for your daughter's education.

"To net $7,200 a year in your 28 percent tax bracket really requires an income of about $10,000 a year to accomplish this goal. If you earned $10,000 and paid 28 percent in taxes, you would have the $7,200 you need to invest; $10,000 times 18 years, means that it would cost you a total of $180,000 to fully finance this goal. You would have to take only $180,000 out of your future income stream to cover this child's educational expenses instead of $490,000!

"We are not talking small potatoes here. We are talking about saving $310,000 or over 63 percent of the total cost of this education program. If you multiply this type of savings by the fact you have two children, not one, then this simple choice of planning can be the total difference of absolute success or total failure in obtaining your all-important goal of retirement. Mr. Langston, can you see how planning makes the difference?"

I was amazed and said, "Yeah, the person who did not plan will take $490,000 out of his future income stream to educate his newborn child, while the person who did plan properly will only use $180,000. And what's more remarkable is that both children will go to the exact same college at the exact same cost, but the person who did the planning will have an extra $310,000 to spend for his other goals. I can really see, Mr. Kane, how a little planning is certainly worth the effort."

"That's very good, Mr. Langston. Investing this $600 a month will cover the cost for the total six years of college with all expenses paid. But if $600 is more than you can afford, you can modify your goals to match your financial capabilities and still help your children. For example, if the child's needs are reduced to four years from six at a cost of $8,000 per year instead of $12,000, the investment cost to finance this program drops from $600 a month to under $260 a month. Make sure you always set your goals according to what you can afford and then, as the popular TV ad for tennis shoes says, 'Just do it!'"

"That's great, Mr. Kane," I said, "but this type of planning program will require a great deal of discipline of me. And unfortunately, Mr. Kane, I am not very good with discipline of this type. I can never stay on my diets, and I must start a new exercise program twice a year."

Mr. Kane looked at me empathetically and said, "In reality, Mr. Langston, implementing this type of plan does not require much discipline at all and is, in fact, very easy."

"Easy?!" I exclaimed. "Give me a break."

"No, really," Mr. Kane continued. "Do you pay your car payment every month?"

"Sure," I said. "I don't want to lose my car."

"Right!" said Mr. Kane. "And how much discipline does that take?"

"None," I answered. "Like I said, I don't want to lose my car."

"And how much is your payment, Mr. Langston?" he asked.

"Around $600 a month," I answered. "I like nice cars."

Mr. Kane then said, "The reason you pay $600 a month for a new car instead of saving for your children's education is that the $600-a-month car is tangible. You can see what you are getting for your money, and at what cost. Goals like retirement and providing college educations are abstract. Most people don't have a clue as to what they need to be doing or how much is enough. The choice shows up as a $600-a-month car payment versus I-do-not-know-what-I-need-to-be-doing. Therefore, if I sacrifice the $600 a month and don't buy the new car, will it really make any difference anyway?

"The beauty of this method, Mr. Langston, is once it is done, the cost of educating your child also becomes a tangible

$600-a-month expense. It then becomes a choice of whether you want a new car or your child's college education. Because you are naturally going to do what you most want to do; whichever you truly want more will win out easily and without effort. If it turns out to be the education, great; if it's the car, tough luck, kid! Once any serious goal is reduced to a tangible cost, it does not require a great deal of discipline or pain to achieve it if you want it more than other things competing for your money."

14

THE HIGHEST AND BEST USE OF YOUR MONEY

As I started thinking about what Mr. Kane had just explained concerning the costs of providing a college education for one's children and what it would take to retire, I began to feel a wave of anxiety. My wife and I were saving a few hundred dollars here and there for the kids' education, but nothing like I could now see we needed to be doing. We were also each contributing a small amount to our 401(k)s, but again, it was now obvious that this was nowhere near enough.

While my wife and I make a respectable income, we were

already spending just about everything we earned. How would we ever be able to earn enough extra money to be able to invest what we needed to meet our goals?

Mr. Kane looked at me and smiled. He once again seemed to know what I was thinking as he said, "Mr. Langston, you looked a bit concerned, so let me ask you if you are worried about how you are going to be able to get the extra amount of money you need to accomplish your financial goals?"

A bit embarrassed, I answered, "Yes, I was just thinking about the fact that we had not been planning properly for our kids' college and our own retirement, and the numbers you just discussed are kind of staggering."

"Yes, Mr. Langston, they are," he agreed. "It will require a lot of new money invested each year to accomplish your financial goals. It will also take real commitment and focus to keep those goals vivid as you continue to make financial choices into the future.

"However, there are many strategies and processes I have revealed to you today that you did not know before that will make this all a lot easier. Plus, there are a few more I would like to share; so let's address both of your current concerns about the new costs you have just learned you need to invest to accomplish your goals, and how to go about finding the extra money you need to do that.

"The next concept is what I call 'always getting the highest and best use of every dollar you spend.'

"Mr. Langston, on the last day of your life, if we had sufficient records to review, we could look back and calculate every dollar that ever came into your possession. This amount would include everything you had ever received from your allowance as a child to every other source of income, gifts, or benefits during your life; and that final amount would be a fixed, finite number. Therefore, we will call this finite number of all revenues received 'your life's income.'

"Additionally, on the last day of your life, if you had never spent a penny of your life's income, you would still have 100 percent of it left. But obviously, since that is not possible, every time you bought something along the way, you were literally removing real dollars from your life's income and replacing those with whatever you spent those dollars on.

"Now, to make my point, if we also on this last day of your life calculated the value of everything you had left, we could instantly see how well you had done in utilizing all the money that had ever come into your possession.

"Therefore, it is of the utmost importance that you become very aware of always getting the highest and best use of every dollar you spend, as this will determine what you have left in your estate of your life's income at your death.

"Every time you buy something, that is an irreversible exchange of that money from your life's income for whatever was purchased. For example, if you go down to the local electronics store and buy a new TV for $1,299, that $1,299 will be removed from your life's income and the TV will replace it. Unfortunately, in this example, the value of that TV in ten years is almost nothing, so there would ultimately be nothing left from the original $1,299.

"Now, what if you shopped around before making this purchase and found that exact same TV set on sale for $999? You would then have the same TV, but you would also have $300 dollars more left from your life's income, which you could use for something else, like possibly investing towards your children's education. If you decided to buy the same version of this TV, but in last year's model instead, you might get it for $799; so now you would have an extra $200 more. Granted, this takes extra effort and time, but how long does it take you to earn $500?

"Now, Mr. Langston, what if you became focused on the importance of always getting the highest and the best use of your money on just about everything you bought, from using dining coupons when you go out to dinner, to using the grocery store's gas rewards program when you fill up your car? Can you see how quickly new money would be found that you are currently let slip through your fingers?"

Once again I was amazed at how a very simple change in the way I currently do things could make such a big difference, as I answered, "I certainly do."

"Good," said Mr. Kane. "Another great way to do this same thing is look through the ads sections in your local Sunday newspaper. The ads you will find there are called *loss leader* sales items, and this is one way stores compete against one another for your business.

"For example, you might see a large office supply chain advertising a $40 box of copy paper for only $26.95 (about their cost). While they don't make any money on the paper if you come in to buy it, they have won the branding war over their competition (which is huge for them); plus, you will probably also buy other things while there at the store that are not on sale.

"Every time you shop for the best deal, instead of just buying on impulse, the extra money you don't spend is now available to use to acquire something else. Mr. Langston, learning to develop a habit of always getting the highest and best use of your money is critical in helping you find the majority of the money you need to invest to meet your financial goals. If you are too proud to use a coupon, drive to a different gas station, or look for a sale, you are squandering a portion of your life's income.

"There is also a new tool that became available around the turn of the century that can help you greatly in getting the highest and best use of your money: the Internet.

"During the majority of my life, this wonderful invention was not available. Therefore, always getting the highest and best use of your money before the Internet was much more difficult than today. Obviously, it was still possible with a lot of work, but because the Internet is the most advanced research facility ever created, finding the best deal now is really very simple if you learn how to use it.

"Shortly after the acceptance of the Internet by the masses, every major and minor store created e-commerce sites to sell their products and services online. Today there is almost nothing you can't buy over the Internet, if you know how to find it.

"Unfortunately, to use the Internet for this purpose requires some initial time to learn how to master researching what you want to buy and who has the best price available on it. Today there are sophisticated search engines that will allow you to easily find the websites of the stores with whom you want to shop, or to locate and compare the price of various products.

"The Internet quickly leveled the playing field for all retailers, as the smallest companies instantly became able to compete on equal footing with the largest. This is because all that is required to sell on the Internet is a good quality website to showcase your wares to potential customers.

"Shortly thereafter, the retailers realized that they were making a lot more money selling to customers online than through their traditional retail stores. This is because there are no retail-related expenses of operations—retail buildings, utilities, property taxes, employees, stocking, pilfering, etc. All that is needed to sell online is a website and a distribution facility. As a result, stores started looking for more and more ways to drive their customers to shop on their websites so they wouldn't have to build so many brick-and-mortar stores.

"The most obvious way to accomplish that was through price reductions. As a result, the same product can now be bought online (even after shipping costs) for less money than in a retail store. This is especially true with many retailers today selling the exact same product cheaper in their online stores than in their brick-and-mortar store.

"It didn't take long before retailers starting using the same types of marketing concepts online they were using in the offline world. One variation of this was the loss leader ads, which now came in the form of what has become known as *banner ads*.

"Banner ads are small ads that appear on other companies' websites wishing to monetize their site. For example, a search engine, blogger, or online newspaper that already had a constant flow of visitors might place a retailer's banner ad alongside their other content, so readers interested in that deal could click on it and go directly to the store's site offering it. If that person then bought something, the original site featuring the ad would receive a commission from the vendor on that sale. Mr. Langston, I suspect you may now notice these types of banner ads on a majority of the websites you regularly visit."

"I sure do," I replied. "Those things are now like TV ads when

I am trying to watch my favorite TV shows; they are cluttering up just about everything I am trying to see on the Internet."

"Yes they are, Mr. Langston," Mr. Kane agreed. "Another method used by retailers trying to attract customers to their online stores is what is known as *promo codes*. Unlike the loss leader sales items offered through the banner ads, which are also available to customers of the online store's site if you looked around for them, promo codes are special discounts only for customers that have the special code, and they cannot be found anywhere on the retailer's website. Think of promo codes as coupons that you take into a store to get a special discount. If you are at the cash register and have the coupon, you pay less for the exact same product than the customer in front of you who did not have the coupon.

"As I said a minute ago, Mr. Langston, the Internet is the best tool I have ever seen for always being able to get the highest and best use of your money. However, learning to use it properly can be a bit complex; and always finding the best deal takes some time to research and find.

"One of the issues with shopping on the Internet is that you have to have the unique web address, or URL, for every store with which you want to shop. This normally means using search engines to locate those URLs, which also means looking through a lot more content than just store names, which takes extra time. Another issue is, how do you find all of the loss leader sale items available online? These appeared on thousands of different websites as banner ads, and unfortunately, there is no such thing as the Sunday newspaper on the Internet that you can look through. The same is true trying to locate all of the promo codes.

"As I researched more about how ecommerce worked, and its driving forces, I started coming up with some ideas of how to create a website to make it much easier for people who wanted to get the highest and best use of their money to be able to do so. One thought I had was, what if there was a giant online shopping mall site, like the Galleria or the Mall of America, that contained all of the best-known retailers on the Internet, all at one single URL? Such a website would allow users to easily access each store's site just like walking through a real mall and walking into their store.

"Then I thought, what if it also could aggregate all of the mall's merchants' loss leader sales items into one place so it was easy to scan all of them and see everything on sale at each store? It could even do the same thing with the mall's stores' promo codes.

"Mr. Langston, the more I researched, the more ideas I had about how to create one website that would be the easiest place on the Internet to find everything you ever needed, from name-brand stores to no-name stores, at the best possible prices. This would be the best tool ever for people who wanted to get the highest and best use of their money."

At that point I realized I had become completely engrossed in what Mr. Kane was explaining. I was actually focusing on each thing he was explaining without thinking ahead, as I normally do. As I began to think about what he was explaining, I could really start to see what he envisioned.

I used the Internet extensively in my line of work with the newspaper, and most of what he explained about shopping I had used in one form or another personally. However, I have never found the Internet convenient enough to make it my primary source of shopping.

One thing that did grab my attention, however, was what Mr. Kane explained about the promo codes. Every time I bought something online, during checkout, just before I entered my credit card information, there was always a spot for me to enter a promo code, which I never had. That kind of infuriated me because I knew someone else who had one was getting a better deal than me. But after looking around the merchant's website for a promo code on several different occasions, and never being able to find one, I finally just gave up and figured I wasn't one of the chosen few.

I could tell Mr. Kane was allowing me to gather my thoughts, so I said, "Mr. Kane, what you are proposing really makes a lot of sense, and I would definitely use such a site if it existed. So what did you ever do with your ideas?"

Mr. Kane replied, "After gathering enough information and fully developing my ideas, I decided to acquire a technology company and build what I envisioned. The site is now fully operational and contains over three thousand major retailers in almost every category you can imagine. You would be hard-pressed to mention any store you can think of by name that isn't available in this Internet mall.

"The mall contains a mall directory, like a real mall, composed of shopping categories (such as Apparel and Shoes, Computers, Electronics, Internet/Phone, Jewelry, Travel, etc.). Using the mall directory, you can find all of the merchants in the mall that sell the type of merchandise you want with a single click or two of your mouse. There is also a sophisticated search engine to allow you to quickly find any store in the mall by its name, or search for what stores sell a specific product you want to buy.

"The mall also has two of my favorite features, which are

called 'Hot Deals' and 'Promo Codes.' The Hot Deals section contains the aggregated content of all of the loss leader sales items of every merchant in the mall. This is like the Sunday newspaper ads on steroids.

"In the Hot Deals section, you can scan all of the deals from all of the stores daily (usually over fifteen hundred to two thousand on any given day), or you can use an alphabet search feature across the top of that section to bring up the stores whose names start with that letter.

"For example, if you wanted to see what Target had on sale today, you would click on the *T* shown in the alphabet stretched across the top of the section, which would bring up all stores that start with the letter *T*. Then you would just scroll down a few stores to Target to see all of their items on sale, with direct links to the page on Target's site that contains that sale item. The Promo Code section works the same way, so you will never again be without the current promo codes available for any store in the mall when you check out."

"Mr. Kane, this sounds really fantastic," I said, "and I really like the idea of making my money go further so I can do more with it. A tool like this would be invaluable in teaching me how to build the habit of thinking ahead before I buy to make sure I always get the best value for my dollar."

Mr. Kane seemed pleased that I saw the value in what he had built and added, "That is good to hear, Mr. Langston. While building this mall, we came across a few additional ways to help people get the most when they shop.

"If you recall, a few minutes ago I explained how Internet stores paid other websites commissions for sending people to their stores. These commissions are an actual percentage of the transaction's purchase price. Since our mall was sending people to the stores in the mall, we were then able to successfully negotiate to receive these same commissions.

"Then we built the technology to track the commissions being received on each transaction, so we could then share a substantial amount of that back with the member that made that purchase. The goal here was to give them an extra reward for using the mall to help them get an even higher and better use of their money. This was money they would not receive from the merchant if they went directly to its store instead. We called this additional payment back to them "cashback." This way, each person that opens a free mall account and then shops with any merchant in the mall receives cashback on their purchase based on what we receive from that merchant. The amount of cashback from a merchant can range from just under 1 percent to as much as 25 percent depending on what the store pays us."

"You mean, if I shop in the mall, not only will it help me find the best deals available, but I will also earn extra cashback I would not receive if I went directly to the store's website to shop?" I asked.

"That's exactly what I mean," Mr. Kane replied. "The goal of the mall is to find every way possible to help people always get the highest and best use of their dollars spent.

"A few years after we launched the initial mall, Facebook and Twitter roared onto the scene, and the viral nature of these networks changed the Internet forever. I was personally fascinated by their success stories, because in the history of business, nothing had ever developed as fast and as large as these two companies. People freely shared Facebook and Twitter with their friends, and never expected or received a cent for doing so. One person simply invited their friends, and those people invited their friends, and so on; and in just five to seven generations down the genealogy chain, there were thousands to hundreds of thousands of people who could be directly traced back to the invitation of that original person.

"And this phenomenon never stopped, as Facebook went from 10,000 members, to 1 million, to 5 million, to 50 million, to 500 million, to over one billion members.

"The more I watched this unfold, in awe, the more ideas started to come to me. Then one day a couple of years later, I started thinking: what would have happened if each of these people on Facebook or Twitter had been rewarded by those companies just a small percentage of what that company was earning from the geometrically expanding network of people that had developed as a result of the friends they invited to join? That amount would have gone a long way toward helping each of them find the extra money they needed to be investing to meet their financial goals.

"This idea wouldn't go away, as I wanted to find a way to harness this type of viral power with our mall, and then reward people for being a part of the growth of what it earned the company. But the problem I kept running up against is our mall was absolutely free; it doesn't charge its members anything to become members. Since we are not charging each member a fee to join the network, how could we then afford to pay each person for helping develop the network?

"Then a couple of years ago I finally figured it out. If the mall was taking a percentage of what we earn from the merchants based on what people buy from them and giving that back to that shopper as cashback, what would happen if we took an extra percentage of our company's earnings from these same transactions and shared that with the person who had invited that shopping member who'd just made the purchase to join; and the person above that who had invited him to join; and so forth, for several generations up the line?

"Mr. Langston, this was a very exciting realization. This meant we could actually create a free viral network that sold nothing, just like Facebook and Twitter. This network in turn would offer its members a significant free value proposition, just like Facebook and Twitter. But unlike those two networks, this network would then reward them for sharing its benefits with their friends.

"Wow! How much faster would Facebook or Twitter have grown if people had been rewarded financially just for sharing it with their friends? That would have been like throwing gasoline on the viral fire that was already blazing away.

"The exciting news for me was that we finally had the concept worked out. So then all that remained was to develop the best business model to share the funds, and then build the technology to be able to do all of this.

"The first part of this equation was not as simple as it sounded. We looked at all kinds of formulas to see how to make this same amount of money that was available to be shared, to become the most possible for everyone involved.

"The initial thoughts gravitated around wanting to give the largest portion of this available money to the person who had referred the shopper, and then give a progressively smaller portion to the referring member in each generation above that. This way you as a referring member could see money developing quickly as the people you invited to join shopped.

"However, no matter what we did in dividing this money up

this way, the amount of extra cashback being set aside to share with the shopping member's genealogy tree above him never really built into anything really significant or exciting.

"For example, if a member earned $5 a month in cashback from their shopping, this new plan called for us to put up an additional $5 from our commission to share with several generations of people above this shopping member. Think of this type of generational development as a family tree: your parent, grandparents, great-grandparents, etc.

"So say we gave 60 percent of that $5 (or $3) to the immediate person that referred the shopping member to become a member of the mall—their first generation, or parent—then gave 10 percent of the $5, or 50 cents each, to both the second and third generations—the shopper's grandparent and great-grandparent—then 5 percent, or 25 cents, to each of the next five generations above that. Doing this would use all 100 percent of the extra $5 allocated to be shared.

"The challenge we kept running into, Mr. Langston, is the development of the genealogy of a family tree is similar to the geometric progression model we discussed earlier: 1 grows to 2, which then grows to 4, which grows to 8, which develops into 16, and so on. The more people you can add to your first generation—your children—the larger the ultimate family number becomes.

"Unfortunately, however, the average person just isn't going to have enough friends to have a lot of people on their first two generations of development to make this available money amount grow to become a lot. Additionally, once you consumed 70 percent to pay the first two generations, the remaining 30 percent was not very exciting when spread thinly with the other generations either.

"We then tried spreading out the percentage on the first few generational levels more evenly to see what that might do; but this still didn't generate super-exciting results either. Then, after several iterations in modeling, it became apparent that we were approaching this completely backwards.

"Instead of paying the vast majority available to the first couple of generations, when you have the smallest number of people in your family tree, and then splitting the remainder with the later ones, we needed to reverse the payout so that we paid the smallest amount on the first several generations and escalated gradually toward the end, so that the majority was paid out on the last generation. This is where you will have the largest population shopping for you due to the genealogy's geometric progression.

"That change blew the number out of the park. This same amount of money being shared this way could now reward everyone involved the most money possible.

"If you think about this, Mr. Langston, it makes complete sense. Would you rather get the largest percentage of money on the smallest number of people in your family tree, your first generations, or on the largest percentage available on your last generations, where geometric progression is magnifying each generation?"

"Of course I would rather have the larger percentage on the larger population," I answered.

"Mr. Kane," I continued, "the Internet mall you have described sounds like a great tool for helping me get the highest and best use of my money on almost everything I need to buy. And just for clarification, you are also saying on top of that I will also earn cashback on every purchase I make, right?"

Mr. Kane started to answer, but I kept talking.

"Plus, I can also share this with my friends so they can shop, save, and earn cashback just like me, and everything is absolutely free for all of us, right?

Before he could respond, I added, "Now on top of this, are you also saying that as my friends shop, save, and earn cashback—plus, when their friends do the same, and their friends' friends, all the way down for seven generations below me—I will earn money each time? . . . Because if all of this is right, this whole thing is an absolute no-brainer!

"So, Mr. Kane, my only question now is, have you already built this genealogy profit-sharing mall model, or is this just something you are still thinking about doing?"

"Mr. Langston, the answer to all of your questions is yes," he replied. "And we just launched this mall a few weeks ago, so please feel free to share that information with the readers of the book you are going to write. The mall is called ShopSaveEarnMoney and can be found at www.ShopSaveEarnMoney.com."

"Mr. Kane, that's fantastic!" I said. "I can't wait to get home and start using it and spreading the word!"

15

THE PROPOSAL

The sun was about to set. The sky was a light blue without a cloud to be seen. Mr. Kane said, "Mr. Langston, this beach is an excellent vantage point to view the sunsets. Watch this sun very closely as it sets. If you are lucky, you will see the okue milahi aloahia, which in Kiki Loaean means, 'the giant green flash.' At the exact moment that the sun disappears below the ocean, if you don't blink, you may see a brilliant green flash of light."

I thought Mr. Kane was pulling my leg, but then realized that everything he had told me today was true, even when at first blush it didn't appear that way. So I watched the sunset with great expectation. The sun was a huge reddish-golden ball. It sank so fast into the horizon that I could actually see the movement. Then, at the exact moment the sun vanished into the sea, I saw it! It was as if a giant green laser had exploded. For a split nanosecond, everything was replaced with a solid sheet of neon green. Then it was gone.

It was truly exhilarating! I felt it deep inside as I also realized that today would change my life forever.

Mr. Kane, as he had repeatedly done all day, read my mind and said, "Mr. Langston, today will become what you make of it. You learned in one day what took me over forty years to learn. But knowledge is of little value if you don't put it to use. Confucius once said, 'To know and not do, is to not know.'

"I selected you, Mr. Langston, because of your intense desire to learn what I know. I now charge you with the responsibility to take what you have learned today and share it with the world. Obtaining wealth is a mind-set. It begins with planting the seeds of your goals in your subconscious mind. And remember: money won't buy happiness, for this is truly a path that should you decide to travel, I promise will not produce positive results."

We walked back to the cab and rode back to the Malihini Hale in silence. My head was so full of information I could barely think.

As Mr. Kane pulled up to the front of the inn, I panicked as I realized I wasn't very good with numbers. Mr. Kane did my daughter's education financial projections in his head. How could I ever get my son's done or my own retirement plan developed? So I said, "Mr. Kane, I am terrible with numbers. I'll never be able to compute these complex financial calculations. You did that stuff back there on the beach in your head. I can't duplicate that."

Once again Mr. Kane smiled his gentle smile and reached in front of me to open the cab's glove box. He took out a thumb drive. As he handed it to me, he said, "This is for you, Mr. Langston."

"What's this for?" I asked. "I'm not a computer expert."

"This, Mr. Langston, is the computer program I personally developed to create the financial projections I provided to my clients," he answered. "I spent over ten years of my life and more than $250,000 in computer programmer's fees perfecting the algorithms contained on this disk. This program will give you the ability to design your children's college education plan. It will also allow you to generate complete actuarial projection, using any variables you wish to use, for your retirement planning. Finally, it will let you determine how much life insurance you need to cover your family's survivorship income needs in the event of your sudden death.

"Mr. Langston, it would take you over a hundred hours of your time to manually duplicate, if you knew how, the projections this computer program will create for you. In fact, I used to charge my clients $5,000 each to prepare a financial plan for them of which these same three financial projections were the principal component.

"But, Mr. Langston, I don't give this program to you solely for your own use. I want you to share it with the world. If you accept this thumb drive, I want you to promise me that you will offer any reader of your book the opportunity for them to send to you their personal goal list. And in return, I want you to generate for them, using this program, their own complete plan of action showing them how to accomplish their children's education goals, as well as their retirement goals, and of course, their family's survivorship income needs."

"But that will take a lot of time and cost me a ton of money!" I protested.

"Yes it will, Mr. Langston. "So charge them a nominal fee to cover your time and overhead, something under $100, because the program will do most of the work for you. That's more than a fair exchange for completely designing a navigable course to the accomplishment of each of their primary financial goals. And Mr. Langston, if you use your time wisely, like I taught you earlier today, maybe you'll hire an assistant to do the computer input, and even make yourself a little profit per case.

"My goal is for anyone who wants a financial plan to be able to obtain one at an affordable cost. When I was accepting clients, only the wealthiest people could afford my $5,000 fee. It is my desire that competent, objective guidance become available through you to anyone who wants it.

"Do you accept my proposal, Mr. Langston?"

"Yes, Mr. Kane, I do," I answered.

16

PASS IT ON

Mr. Kane and I got out of the cab, and I didn't know what to say. Finally, I managed, "Mr. Kane, the words escape me. I don't know how to thank you. You have provided me with so much more than I ever imagined possible."

"It was my pleasure, Mr. Langston," he replied. "I know you will be a good steward of what I have entrusted to you today. It is time for me to leave now. I will pick you up tomorrow morning at 4:30 to go watch the sunrise, and then take you to the airport."

I didn't sleep at all that night. I kept going over and over in my mind all that I had learned that day. I was still awake when my travel alarm announced the arrival of 4:00 a.m.

Mr. Kane arrived, just the same as the morning before, exactly at 4:30. We drove to the same site and watched a glorious sunrise. I thanked God for steering me to Mr. Kane and realized that I now had a new mission in life. It was now my job to spread the financial gospel according to Mr. Kane.

When we got back to the airport, I thanked Mr. Kane again and then asked him the question I had been dying to ask him since I first read he was worth $20 billion. "Mr. Kane, please don't think me rude, but you are one of the richest men in the world. Why do you choose to drive a cab on this tiny island for a living?"

Mr. Kane's smile grew as large as his face as he looked me in the eye and said, "My dear Mr. Langston, I thought the answer to that question would be obvious to you by now. I worked hard to rebuild the fortune I lost in my thirties, and by the time I was fifty, I was a billionaire. As I told you, I learned on the first go-round that money doesn't buy happiness. In fact, for me, I am the happiest when I am contributing to someone else.

"When I designed my new set of goals in my early forties, after my fall, many of those goals had to do with creating foundations to help the homeless, the hungry, and abused children. The reason I worked so hard to build my net worth so high the second time was to give me the ability to really do something significant in those areas.

"On my sixtieth birthday I retired, according to my goals, and came back to Kiki Loa. I didn't want to sit around and do nothing, so I thought about what I really like to do most in the world. The answer is to be with people and to drive around this beautiful island and witness the glory of one of God's most beautiful creations. So I bought a cab in the States and had it shipped here and became a cabbie. Today, Mr. Langston, I am the happiest I have ever been in my life. And you know what? I spend almost no money on myself. I truly hope that you can plan your life so that one day you can experience the same sense of satisfaction."

Epilogue

I returned to the States and wrote Mr. Kane's story, *Billionaire Cab Driver*, which you obviously have just read. I also began following Mr. Kane's advice. I start early every morning taking a walk around my neighborhood and watch the sunrise. Using Mr. Kane's computer program, I also defined all my goals, including retirement, my children's educational needs, and my family's survivorhip income needs in the event of my unexpected death. I also set many nonmonetary goals, including a good health program, great family relationships, and of course, charitable giving not only of my money, but more satisfying to me, my time.

And of course, I kept my promise to Mr. Kane and created

a way for everyone to be able to develop an affordable, objective financial plan. Originally, I created a financial planning service and made it available by mail for a cost of only $99.99 (I stayed under his desired $100 maximum). But with the advancements in the Internet and technology, we have been able to take Mr. Kane's software and build a website where anyone can now come and, for a much smaller fee, use the software to create their own financial plan.

And in keeping true to Mr. Kane's intent and my promise to him, due to the automation of the website, we have also been able to lower the cost of building one of these financial plans down to only $29.95.

If you would like to have access to this software, visit http:// BillionaireCabDriver.com. There you can access the software and develop your own financial plan containing all the philosophies and financial projections covered in this book to enable you to begin the journey to obtaining the financial future you want. Good luck! I hope you achieve your every goal. I know I am finally accomplishing mine.

About the Author

Joseph "Jody" Tallal, Jr. is a man of many talents and interests. A personal financial manager to wealthy professionals, Tallal became one of the first fee only advisors in the 1970s. His success led to developing a course to train medical professionals at Baylor Medical School, University of Tennessee Health Sciences, and Tulane Medical School on how to manage their money.

Mr. Tallal is the author of two books and numerous articles which have been published in major periodicals including *Barron's, Southern Banker, Financial Services Times, American Banker, Inc. Magazine,* and *The Magazine,* the official inflight magazine of Southwest Airlines. Mr. Tallal is also the author of the Nightingale Conant audio/video program, Building Personal Wealth, has been interviewed on many radio and television shows and hosted his own financial planning radio talk show.

A nationally acclaimed personal financial manager, Mr. Tallal has been an advisor to wealthy individuals for more than a third of a century. He has been named an Honorary Citizen by several city mayors nationwide and has also received the President's Medal of Merit from former president Ronald Reagan. In 1981, he served on the Chairman's Committee of the United States Senatorial Business Advisory Board.